THE WORLD MIDDLEWEIGHT PUNCHERS HALL OF FAME

By
Larry Carli

The World Middleweight Punchers Hall of Fame

ISBN: 978-1-61170-326-9

Back Cover Photo: Rocky Graziano vs. Tony Zale
  Boxing International All-Star Wrestling, July 1965

Published by:

Rp **Robertson Publishing**™
www.RobertsonPublishing.com

Printed in the USA and UK on acid-free paper.

To purchase additional prints of this book go to:
  amazon.com
  barnesandnoble.com

Larry Carli has also written:
- *1950's Boxing in Black and White*
- *Boxing's Super 70's*
- *The Top Ten Middleweight Champions of All Time: Who Was The Greatest?*

Preface

In this book, you will read about the most powerful punchers in the middleweight division covering a period of over 100 years from Bob Fitzsimmons in the 1890's to Gennady Golovkin in 2022.

All of the fighters that I have selected over this 100 year time period had a knockout to win ratio of over 75 per cent.

Of the 15 punchers that I have selected only 11 of them were world champions and 2 of the fighters were never given a shot at a world title.

Though some of the fighters were not world champions, all of them were Hall of Fame punchers who could take an opponent out with just one punch.

Have fun reading this book and compare your own selections to the power punchers that I have chosen in this book for the hall of fame.

Table of Contents

Bob Fitzsimmons
The Legendary Champions, by Rex Lardner, 1972

Inductee # 1   BOB FITZSIMMONS

Bob Fitzsimmons was born on June 4, 1864 in Cornwall, England. At the age of 9 his family migrated to Lyttleton on the East Coast of New Zealand's South Island At the local school "Fitz" became a star sprinter and soccer player.

At an early age he was apprenticed as a blacksmith and earned his muscles by pounding a sledgehammer on an anvil to shape sizzling sections of iron.

When Fitzsimmons was 18, famed boxing bare knuckle legend Jem Mace came to New Zealand to supervise an amateur boxing tournament. Weighing approximately 140 pounds the freckled Fitzsimmons entered the Heavyweight divison of the tournament and proceeded to knockout 4 separate local boxers to become the Heavyweight Champion of New Zealand.

Turning professional Fitzsimmons beat his first 3 opponents and then looked for greener pastures by stowing away on a Two masted scooner bound for Sydney, Australia.

Under the tuteledge of Jem Mace, Fitzsimmons learned how to put leverage in his punches and he became a terrific body puncher. Fitzsimmons had close to 30 professional fights in Australia, winning the Australian Middleweight title from Jim Hall, and then losing it to Hall in a rematch for the title.

Fitzsimmons now had enough money to book passage to San Francisco, California, and fight out of the prestigous California Athletic Club. When Fitzsimmons arrived at the California athletic club he was laughed at by the club members because of his huge upper body, and spindly looking legs. It was said that he had the upper torso of a heavyweight and the lower torso of a lightweight. To make matters worse Fitzsimmons was heavily freckled which gave his body a reddish complexion, and he was given the nickname of "Ruby Robert" due to his unlikely appearance.

Fitzsimmons was first matched with a hard hitting middleweight named Frank Allen in May of 1900. Fitzsimmons jabbed at Allen and then threw a short explosive right hand that sent Allen rolling on the floor. Allen broke his wrist when he landed and Fitzsimmons was awarded a TKO victory. The California Athletic Club members no longer laughed at Fitzsimmons physical appearance.

Fitzsimmons next opponent was an Australian named Billy McCarthy who was considered the top contender to middleweight champion Jack (Nonpereil) Dempsey, who is not to be confused with the future heavyweight champion, Jack Dempsey.

McCarthy made the mistake of poking fun of Fitzsimmon's appearance. Fitzsimmons then proceeded to give McCarthy a systematic beating before finally knocking him out in the 9th round.

In June of 1890 Fitzsimmons demolished one Arthur Upham in 5 rounds at the New Orleans Audobon Club. Promoters immediately matched Fitzsimmons with World Middlewieght Champion Dempsey with a fight to the finish for the world title at the Olympic Club in New Orleans in January of 1891.

Dempsey had held the world title for over 7 years, and he was considered to be a courageous, tricky, and popular champion. It would later be said that Dempsey did not train properly for his title defense and that he had underestimated Fitzsimmons as a challenger.

Fitzsimmons was in top shape for the title fight and he outboxed and cut up Dempsey over the first 12 rounds of the fight. When Fitzsimmons corner advised him that Dempsey's corner was ready to stop the fight, Fitzsimmons dashed out of his corner for the 13th round and drove Dempsey into the ropes. Fitzsimmons then knocked Dempsey out cold with a straight right hand blow to the head. Rumor had it that Fitzsimmons then helped carry Dempsey to his corner after the knockout.

As middleweight champion Fitzsimmons found that there was no real money to be made and he therefore started looking for fights in the heavyweight divion. In the 1890's the lightheavyweight divison did not exist. Fitzsimmons was greatly encouraged by his new manager Martin Julian, and Julian's sister Rose to go after the bigger purses which meant a foray into the heavyweight division. The management team became inseperable, and Fitzsimmons would soon make Rose his wife.

After a couple of tuneup fights, Fitzsimmons, at around 165 pounds, took on ranking heavyweight Peter Maher of Ireland in March of 1892. Maher was 6 feet tall, and weighed around 200 pounds. Even though Fitzsimmons was greatly outweighed he chose to slug it out with his heavier opponent. Maher welcomed the challenge but Fitzsimmons' punches were faster and more accurate. Fitzsimmons cornered Maher in the 12th round and knocked him out with a left hook to the jaw and a powerful straight right hand to the body.

In April of 1892 Fitzsimmons went on a tour of Newark, New Jersey, and knocked out 3 separate opponents, none of which lasted 4 rounds with him.

In March of 1893 Fitzsimmons decided to defend his middleweight title and he knocked out Jim Hall at the Crescent City Club in New Orleans, Louisiana.

In May of 1894 Fitzsimmons took on fellow hard punching heavyweight Joe Choynski in Boston, Massachusetts, in a 5-round match. In the 3rd round Choynski dropped Fitzsimmons with a straight hard right hand to the head. Fitzsimmons lasted out the round and came out for the 4th round enraged; he immediately starting battering Choynski at will until the police came in and stopped the fight. Since no one had been knocked out by the finish of the fight, the match was called a draw.

Fitzsimmons defended his middleweight title for the last time by knocking out previously undefeated challenger Dan Creedon in New Orleans in September of 1894.

In February of 1896 Fitzsimmons was matched with Peter Maher for a bout being billed as a heavyweight title fight. The true heavyweight champion was Jim Corbett, but at the time Corbett was not accepting any challenges to his title.

Fitzsimmons had previously knocked out Maher in 1892, but accepted the rematch due to the championship billing. The fight took place across the border from Langtry Texas, on Mexican soil. Since Fitzsimmons was denied any rights to the filming of the match, he decided to knock Maher out quickly. Fitzsimmons ducked a long left hand from Maher and countered with a hard right to Mahers jaw. Maher fell, and rolled over on his back where he took the 10-count half way through the first round.

Fitzsimmons was then matched with 'Sailor" Tom Sharkey with the winner promised a title match with champion Jim Corbett. The fight took place in December of 1896 and the referee was the legendary old west lawman, Wyatt Earp.

Fitzsimmons easily outboxed Sharkey in the early rounds, before he drove home a powerful body punch that send Sharkey to the floor, clutching his groin and hollering that he had been fouled. Even though the body blow appeared to be above the belt line, Earp bought Sharkey's act, disqualified Fitzsimmons for a low blow, and awarded the unpopular verdict to Sharkey.

The public did not buy Earp's decision to disqualify Fitzsimmons, therefore Fitzsimmons was given the title match against Corbett, instead of Sharkey.

Jim Corbett brought style and elegance to boxing and was nicknamed "Gentleman Jim". Corbett looked down upon Fitzsimmons and felt that he was a "freaky looking brawler" who would never be able to beat him. Corbett, in general, felt that Fitzsimmons was an unworthy opponent and that the public would not pay to see such a fight.

After a lot of legal haggling, the match was finally set for March 17th, 1897, in Carson City, Nevada. The boxing promoters immediately billed the title fight, as "the battle of the century". No fight before this had such massive publicity and national coverage. It was also held in the first outdoor arena erected especially for a prize fight. It was also the first heavyweight title fight to ever be recorded on film.

Champion Corbett weighed in at 183 pounds for the contest and was 6'1" in height. Corbett also appeared to be in excellent physical condition. Fitzsimmons weighed in at 167 pounds and was 5'11". By todays standards, Fitzsimmons was little more then a super-middleweight. Looking at Fitzsimmons, it was obvious that his massive upper torso, due to his early days as a blacksmith, did not match his thin spindly legs. Before the fight, at ring center, Fitzsimmons refused to shake hands with Corbett due to all the insults Corbett threw at him in the build up to the fight.

The fight began and Corbett easily controlled the first 6 rounds with his jabs and superior boxing skills. Corbett cut up and bloodied Fitzsimmons face with his rapier like jabs, flooring his opponent in the 6th round with a left hook. Fitzsimmons got up bloody and barely beat the 10-count. The bell rang ending the round right after Fitzsimmons was upright. Fitzsimmons, with his amazing recuperative powers, came out fresh for the 7th round and hurt Corbett for the first time with a left hand to the stomach which caused Corbett to backpedal to avoid more damage.

Fitzsimmons wins the title from Corbett in 1897
The Legendary Champions, by Rex Lardner, 1972

Fitzsimmons, with blood streaming down his face from several cuts, plodded after Corbett who appeared to be tiring by the 8th round. Finally in the 14th round, with Corbett protecting his face, Fitzsimmons landed a powerful left hook to the pit of Corbett's stomach, which caused him to collapse to the ring floor. Corbett was conscious but was unable to control his lower limbs to climb from the canvas. At the count of 8, Corbett reached for a ring rope but missed the rope and fell on his face until the count of 10. The bloodied Fitzsimmons was now an unlikely new heavyweight champion of the world. When Corbett finally arose from the canvas, he had to be restrained from getting at Fitzsimmons as he seemed to be unaware that he had just lost his title. Corbett asked for a rematch but Fitzsimmons told Corbett that he would never fight him again, and Fitzsimmons kept his word never entering into a ring with Corbett for his entire career.

For the next 2 years, Fitzsimmons and his wife Rose would tour the country in a play that was especially written for them by playwright William Gill titled "The Honest Blacksmith". During the play Fitzsimmons would demonstrate his Blacksmith skills onstage, and then talk to his audiences during the later stages of the performance.

In 1899 Fitzsimmons finally defended his title against a bear of a man named James J. Jeffries who had been a sparring partner for the former champion, Jim Corbett. The fight took place in Coney Island, New York, in June of 1899. Jeffries was 6'2" in height, and weighed a muscular 206 pounds for the fight. Fitzsimmon came in at his normal 167 pounds for the title defense.

The fight began and Fitzsimmons powerful blows had barely any effect on Jeffries who was fighting out of a defensive crouch. Jeffries eventually sprung to life in the 11th round and knocked out an exhausted Fitzsimmons with a vicious left hook to the head and a right uppercut to the point of the chin.

Fitzsimmons eventually regrouped and knocked out heavyweight contenders Gus Ruhlin and Tom Sharkey in a rematch to earn a return match for the title with Jim Jeffries in July of 1902 in San Francisco, California.

It was rumored that Fitzsimmons used plaster of paris inside of his gloves which hardened quickly and added more force to his blows. Because of this advantage, he opened hideous cuts all over Jeffries face in the first 7 rounds of the fight. By today's standards, the fight would have been stopped for a TKO win for Fitzsimmons. But in 1902 the fight continued and a desperate Jeffries came out for the 8th round bleeding profusely with his left eye closed. Jeffries wasted little time in cornering Fitzsimmons and drove a hard left hand to the liver which dropped Fitzsimmons to the canvas for the full 10-count. Fitzsimmons had come very close to becoming the first heavyweight champion to ever regain his title.

Fitzsimmons would never fight for the heavyweight title again, but in November of 1903 he was matched with George Gardner for a newly created Lightheavyweight title. Fitzsimmons won a 20 round decision over Gardner to become the first boxer in ring history to have won world titles in 3 separate weight divisions.

Fitzsimmons would lose the lightheavyweight title to Philadelphia Jack O'Brien in 1905. Fitzsimmons would continue fighting until the age of 50 when he won decisions over Dan Sweeney and Jersey Bellow in 1914.

Fitzsimmons died of pneumonia in 1917. His final ring record was 61 wins, 8 losses, and 4 draws. He won 57 fights by knockout giving him a kayo to win percentage of 93.4 per cent. He was listed as the 8th greatest puncher of all time, by the 2003 Ring Magaine editon of the 100 greatest punchers of all time.

Fitzsimmons was one of the few middleweights in ring history who could knockout an opponent with a single blow. He was inducted into the International Boxing Hall of Fame in 1990.

Charles (Kid) McCoy
The Ring Magazine 2003 Yearbook; The 100 Greatest Punchers

Inductee # 2 CHARLES (KID) McCOY

Charles (Kid) McCoy was born Norman Selby on October 13, 1872, in Moscow, Indiana. Selby quit school as a teenager and, like Stanley Ketchel and Jack Dempsey, he became a hobo riding the rails across the country. Selby gained his amateur fighting experience fighting with railway cops and other hobos on the trains.

As legend would have it, Selby is credited with inventing the "corkscrew punch." He claimed in later years that he got the idea of twisting his hand at the end of a jab which would rip the skin open on an opponent. Selby also claimed he also observed cats doing the same thing by striking with their paws at an angle when attacking.

When Selby was finally detained by railway police, he claimed he gave them the name of Charles McCoy. What is a known fact is that Selby turned professional at the age of 18 under the name Charles (Kid) McCoy in St. Paul, Minnesota, by winning a 4-round decision over Peter Jenkins on June 1, 1891.

McCoy was a lean figure in the ring at nearly 6 feet tall and weighing between 150 and 160 pounds. McCoy traveled all over the eastern and southern part of the United States taking on all comers with his slashing fists.

McCoy was undefeated in his first 15 fights and did not taste defeat until he was surprised in the first round by Billy Steffers in

11

May of 1894 in Cleveland, Ohio. McCoy defeated Steffers in a rematch in Cleveland in July of 1894 and also won their rubber match by decision in August of 1894. McCoy gained national recognition when he gave a severe 10 round beating to a rugged Australian named "Shadow" Billy Maber in March of 1895 in Memphis, Tennessee.

McCoy then became a sparring partner for world welterweight champion Tommy Ryan. McCoy learned to dislike Ryan for the severe beating that Ryan gave him and the rest of his sparring partners when in training for his title defenses.

After going undefeated in his next 7 fights, McCoy asked Ryan for a title fight for the vacant middleweight title when he was at a fighting weight of 154 pounds. As legend would have it, McCoy feigned illness and advised Ryan that, besides being sick, he was also broke and in bad need of a payday. Ryan eventually agreed to the title fight and supposedly did not train very hard for his fight with McCoy.

McCoy and Ryan fought in March of 1896 in the Queens section of New York City. McCoy gave the out of shape Ryan a severe beating in every round of the fight and could have finished him early but decided to extend his misery for 15 rounds before knocking him out with a right hand to the head. At the age of 22 McCoy claimed the vacant middleweight title and perched it cockily on top of his head.

In May of 1896 McCoy retained his title by a 6-round disqualification against Mysterious Billy Smith in Boston, Massachusetts, and then sailed to Johannesburg, South Africa in December of 1896 to knock out Bill Doherty in 9 rounds and claim the middleweight title of South Africa after the contest.

Several months later and back in the United States, McCoy went on a lengthy unbeaten streak slashing away at his opponents with his famed "Corkscrew punch".

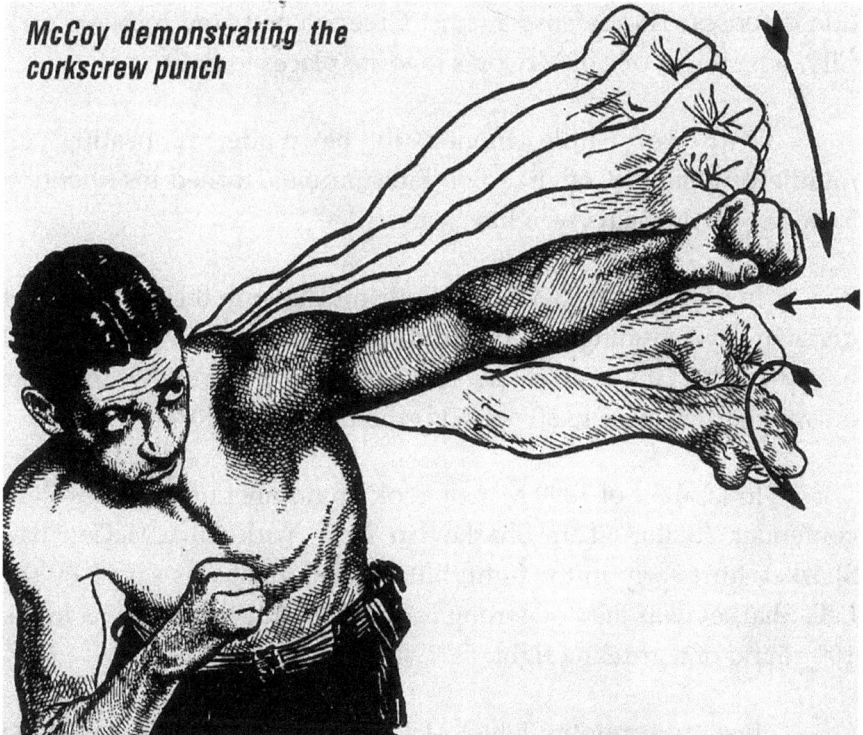

McCoy demonstrating the corkscrew punch

The Ring Magazine 2003 Yearbook; The 100 Greatest Punchers

By this time in his life McCoy had already married and divorced twice while traveling around the country taking on all comers and defending his title, on occasion, when challenged.

In September of 1897 McCoy finally gave Ryan a rematch, but referee George Siler called the 5 round bout a draw because he saw no reason for the police to have intervened in the fight. The police, led by an Inspector O'Brien claimed that they had been ordered to do so by the mayor if they saw any inappropriate fighting.

In December of 1897 he was finally challenged again for his middleweight title by Dan Creedon. McCoy easily stopped Creedon and cut his face to ribbons in the 15th round of a scheduled 25 round fight with his slashing "corkscrew punch". Ring observers reported that McCoy could have stopped Creedon any time after the 10th round, but the champion was especially hard on challengers during title defenses. The defense against Creedon occurred in New York City, which was one of McCoy's favorite places to fight.

With very little money to be made in beating up middleweights, McCoy, like Bob Fitzsimmons, turned his attention to taking on the heavyweights.

In March of 1898 McCoy made his debut in the heavyweight division by winning a 20-round decision over top ten rated heavyweight Gus Ruhlin in Syracuse, New York. McCoy was outweighed by close to 50 pounds when he fought Ruhlin.

In January of 1899 McCoy took on number one heavyweight contender "Sailor" Tom Sharkey in New York City. McCoy had Sharkey hurt early in the fight, but his opponent was saved by the bell. Sharkey was just too strong for McCoy and stopped him in the 10th round of a grueling fight.

Just two months later, McCoy took on another top-rated heavyweight in San Francisco named Joe Choynski. McCoy won a hard fought 20 round decision over Choynski in his hometown.

McCoy gave Choynski a rematch in Chicago, Illinois, in October of 1899, where they fought to a 6-round draw. On New Year's Day in 1900, McCoy celebrated the new year by knocking out another top heavyweight contender in Peter Maher. After knocking out Maher in the 5th round, McCoy made all the stops at his favorite night clubs to celebrate while in New York City.

McCoy began clamoring for a heavyweight title fight with champion Jim Jeffries, but no promoter could be found that wanted to put the scrawny middleweight in with the heavyweight champion of the world. Instead of fighting Jeffries, McCoy found himself knocking out old foe Joe Choynski in a rubber match in 4 rounds on January 12, 1900, while he was still in New York City.

In May of 1900 McCoy knocked out Dan Creedon again in 6 rounds and fought a 6-round draw with his old sparring partner, the ex-champion Tommy Ryan.

On June 1st of 1900, McCoy received another challenge to his world middleweight title from contender Jack Bonner. McCoy easily dispatched Bonner in 13 rounds in New York City. In August of 1900 McCoy was matched with former heavyweight champion Jim Corbett in New York City. In a fight where neither fighter seemed to be trying too hard to win, Corbett was awarded a 5th round technical knockout victory.

McCoy then took a year off from boxing to party and get involved in several more marriages before sailing to England in December of 1901 to win several fights. McCoy then returned to the United States to take on Fred Russell and Kid Carter in May of 1902 in Philadelphia, Pennsylvania. Both of McCoy's fights in Philadelphia ended up in newspaper decisions.

In April of 1903 McCoy faced Jack Root for the inaugural world light heavyweight title in Detroit, Michigan. McCoy lost a close 10 round decision to Root.

McCoy took another year off from boxing and eventually returned to the ring in April of 1904 to take on novice heavyweight Henry Placke in Philadelphia, Pennsylvania. McCoy was outweighed by close to 100 pounds, but he made a bloody mess of Placke before the referee mercifully stopped the contest in the 2nd round. In May of 1904 McCoy fought to a 6 round newspaper draw with Philadelphia Jack O'Brien in O'Briens hometown.

In September of 1904 McCoy won a 20-round decision over

top middleweight contender Jack "Twin" Sullivan in Los Angeles, California. After a lengthy absence from the ring, to get involved in more marriages, McCoy finally returned and knocked out old heavyweight opponent Peter Maher in 2 rounds with the famed "corkscrew punch" in New York City.

In 1911 McCoy knocked out Kid Elle in 1 round, and Jim Savage in 4 rounds in New York City. McCoy wished to end his career fighting in France.

In December of 1911 McCoy knocked out Harry Croxon in 3 rounds in Paris, and on January 10th he won a 10-round decision over George Gunther in Paris. McCoy concluded his career by winning a 20-round decision over P.O. Matthew Curran in Nice, France.

What was incredible was that McCoy won the last 13 fights of his career after his 1903 loss to Jack Root. McCoy was close to 40 years old when he retired, and he was still winning fights by knockout with his famed "corkscrew punch." McCoy was also unbeaten in the last 9 years of his ring career.

During World War 1, McCoy was a one-man bond drive as he sold certificates to support Uncle Sam. McCoy also served a one-year hitch with the 29th infantry division even at his advanced age.

McCoy's name stayed in the headlines even after his ring career was over due to his various marriages and acting in some of Hollywood's best blood and thunder action-adventure movies.

In the 1920's McCoy again made headlines in a negative way. In 1924 McCoy moved in with a woman he had met who was going through a divorce. After a lengthy argument, McCoy was accused of shooting his roommate in the head.

After the woman's body was found, McCoy was arrested a few blocks away, running and carrying a pistol. McCoy was arrested and went on trial for murder. The jury was deadlocked on the murder charge, but he was ultimately convicted of manslaughter. McCoy received a sentence of 24 years to be served at San Quentin prison in California.

McCoy began serving his sentence in 1925 and he was paroled for good behavior in 1932. Upon his release, McCoy obtained employment with the Ford Motor company in Detroit, Michigan.

On one of his trips back home to Rushville, Indiana, McCoy meet his 8th wife, the former Sue Cobb Cowley, a cousin of a famous humorist at the time Irving S. Cobb.

McCoy seemed to have everything going his way with a steady job and happy marriage. People would continually ask him for an autograph or wanted to shake the old prize fighter's hand.

On the cold dreary morning of April 18th, 1940, a detective and hotel manager were looking at a man's body who had just committed suicide by overdosing on sleeping pills at the Hotel Tuller in Detroit, Michigan. The man left a suicide note which said "everything in my possession I want to go to my dear wife Sue E. Selby…to all my dear friends, best of luck, sorry I could not endure this world's madness" Norman Selby.

Whatever Norman Selby a.k.a. Kid McCoy did in his lifetime, he was always in the headlines.

There are various statistics for McCoy's actual final ring record, but it is generally agreed that the following is a good estimate: 74 wins, 6 losses, and 9 draws. 59 wins by knockout for a knockout to win percentage of 79.7 per cent.

McCoy was listed as the 74th greatest puncher of all time by the Ring magazine's 2003 issue of the 100 greatest punchers of all time. He was inducted into the International Boxing Hall of fame in 1991.

Stanley Ketchel
The Ring Magazine 2003 Yearbook; The 100 Greatest Punchers

Inductee # 3   *STANLEY KETCHEL*

Stanley Ketchel was born on September 14, 1886, in Grand Rapids, Michigan, as Stanislaus Kiecal. Ketchel was of Polish descent and was later nicknamed "The Michigan Assassin" during his ring career due to his explosive punching power.

As a youngster, Ketchel left Michigan and "rode the rails" and lived life as a hobo before settling in as a bouncer in saloons in Butte, Montana.

Ketchel developed a reputation as a tough 140-pound bouncer and at the urging of friends, he turned professional as Stanley Ketchel in May of 1903, instead of his birth name of Kiecel

When asked about his amateur boxing experience, Ketchel replied that he learned to fight knocking out 200-pound drunks in the saloons of Butte, Montana.

Ketchel's professional debut was on May 2, 1903, when the wild swinging Ketchel knocked out Kid Tracy in one round. Maurice Thompson, a boxing coach in the area and a professional fighter, wished to train Ketchel and teach him the finer points of boxing, but the headstrong Ketchel declined the offer but agreed to fight Thompson in a 6-round match.

Thompson easily outpointed the crude punching Ketchel by simply jabbing and dancing around the ring in a boring fight.

Ketchel then went on a 7-fight knockout spree which included wins over Jimmy Quinn, Jim McGuire, Kid Leroy, Johnny Murray, and Johnny Gilsey. Ketchel felt that, after his run of wins, he was ready to reverse his loss to Thompson, and he challenged him to another 6-round match.

Ketchel fought Thompson again in October of 1904 and again lost the 6 round decision as he was unable to corner the jabbing and running Thompson.

Under managers Joe O'Conner and Willis Britt, Ketchel was able to learn some boxing skills to go along with his tremendous right hand punching power.

Ketchel then went on a 4-fight winning streak by knocking out Jimmy Kelly, Kid Foley, Joe Mudro, and Kid Herrick. In December of 1904, Ketchel again challenged Maurice Thompson to a 10-round match and agreed that if both men were still standing at the end of 10 rounds, the match would be declared a no-contest.

Thompson accepted the challenge and Ketchel battered Thompson around the ring for the whole 10 rounds but was unable to knock out the running opponent. As there was no knockout, the bout was declared a no-contest.

Beginning in 1905 Ketchel matured as a fighter as he learned to slip opponents punches, by using a bob and weave type of defense, and improved his counter punching skills. Ketchel also learned to cut off the ring when stalking his opponents inside of the ring.

Ketchel went undefeated in 17 straight fights in 1905 recording 16 wins by knockout and fighting 1 draw. Ketchel defeated top middleweight contenders Kid Thomas, Jerry McCarthy, and Kid Fredericks during his winning streak.

Ketchel would go undefeated in his next 5 fights in Montana in 1906 before leaving for the greener pastures of California in his pursuit for a world boxing title.

In March of 1907 Ketchel arrived in California and knocked out Mike McClure in Redding. In May of 1907 Ketchel knocked out Benny Hart in Marysville, and followed it with knocking out George Brown in Sacramento, California.

On July 4, 1907, Ketchel challenged number 1 welterweight and middleweight contender Joe Thomas in Marysville, California. Ketchel and Thomas fought viciously to a draw decision and a rematch was in order.

In September of 1907 Ketchel knocked out Thomas at a weight of 150 pounds in Colma, California and claimed the world middleweight title.

In December of 1907 Ketchel won a decision over Thomas in San Francisco and he was generally recognized as the world middleweight champion

In February of 1908 Ketchel knocked out Mike (Twin) Sullivan in Colma, California in 1 round, and then knocked out his brother Jack (Twin) Sullivan in 20 rounds to gain universal recognition as world middleweight champion

In June of 1908 Ketchel won a hard fought 10 round decision over an up-and-coming rough neck contender from Illinois, named Billy Papke. Papke, like Ketchel, was an aggressive battler who never took a backward step, and the match was close and fought at close quarters for the whole bout.

Ketchel was a champion who took on all contenders and in July of 1908 he defended his title by knocking out perennial contender Hugo Kelly in 3 rounds in San Francisco, California.

In August of 1908 Ketchel fought Joe Thomas for the 4th time in his career. Ketchel was able to easily knock Thomas out, thus ending his career as a middleweight title threat.

The boxing public was clamoring for Ketchel to defend his title against the number one middleweight contender, Billy Papke, who was nicknamed "the Illinois Thunderbolt." Ketchel eventually agreed to defend his title against the Illinois challenger in September of 1908 in Vernon, California. Former heavyweight champion Jim Jeffries agreed to referee the middleweight title contest.

Newspapers reported that after the fighters came to ring center to begin the contest, Ketchel actually threw the first punch. After the first real exchange seconds into the start of the fight, Ketchel found himself bleeding and sitting on the ring canvas. Some accounts of the fight claimed that Papke struck Ketchel when he went to shake hands before the start of the contest

Ketchel arose from the canvas, groggy, after the first knockdown. Ketchel took a vicious pounding in the first round and went down several times before the bell rang to end the round. Ketchel returned to his corner with one eye closed and blood coming from his nose and mouth.

Over the course of the next 10 rounds Ketchel took a vicious beating and tried fighting back in his weakened condition. Ringsiders screamed for Jeffries to stop the fight, but the former champion allowed the fight to continue. Finally in the 12th round, after taking a hard right hand from Papke, Ketchel fell to the canvas in a sitting position and was unable to rise before the 10-count. At the end of the bloody encounter, Ketchel's eyes were closed, and he had sustained a broken nose.

After the fight, Papke claimed that he did not foul Ketchel and that when fighting a man like him you had to be prepared to fight as soon as the first bell rang.

Ketchel was a tough, hard, and mean fighter, and within two months his wounds were healed, and he was ready to take on Papke in a return match. Ketchel never complained about Papke fouling him in the first fight and just stated that he would be ready to fight as soon as the first bell sounded.

The rematch between the two warriors took place on the 26th of November in 1908, Thanksgiving Day in Colma, California. This time there was no handshake before the start of the contest.

Both fighters started out aggressively, but Ketchel fought like a demon and took everything that Papke had to offer, and counter punched him viciously. Ketchel continually beat Papke to the punch and dropped him at the end of the first round.

During the middle rounds, it seemed like Ketchel could have stopped Papke any time that he wanted, and it appeared that he seemed to enjoy the beating he was giving his rival. In the 11th round Ketchel got serious about his work and dropped Papke near the ropes with a vicious uppercut to the chin which dropped his rival on the seat of his shorts. Papke was still flat on his back when the referee counted 10 over him. Ketchel thus became the first middleweight champion in ring history to ever regain his title.

In March of 1909 Ketchel took on light heavyweight champion Philadelphia Jack O'Brien in New York City. O'Brien easily out boxed the plodding Ketchel in the early rounds and had a large lead on points. Ketchel started to come on in the later stages of the fight, and with 5 seconds to go before the final bell, he connected with O'Brien's jaw knocking him out cold. When the final bell rang, O'Brien had to be dragged to his corner by his seconds. Ketchel was given the newspaper decision, but the title did not change hands.

Ketchel fought a rematch with O'Brien in June of 1909 in Philadelphia. Ketchel knocked out the aging O'Brien but never laid claim to the old warrior's light heavyweight title. Ketchel had instead set his sights on Heavyweight champion Jack Johnsons title.

Before Ketchel took on Johnson he agreed to a fourth match with his middleweight nemesis Billy Papke. The fight with Papke took place in July of 1909 in Colma, California.

The fourth fight with Papke could have been held in a telephone booth. Both fighters fought non-stop for 20 rounds with both bleeding heavily. Neither fighter gave ground during the fight, and it was a very close fight. As champion, the decision went to Ketchel, thus ending their 4-bout series.

In October of 1909 Ketchel was finally awarded a title fight with heavyweight champion Jack Johnson in Colma, California. At well over 6 feet tall, and over 200 pounds, Johnson towered over the 5'9" Ketchel who weighed less then 170 pounds for the contest. It has been written, but never proved, that both fighters agreed to just fight to a draw in order to draw a larger gate for a bigger match for the title.

Ketchel knocking down champion Jack Johnson in 1909
The Ring Magazine 2003 Yearbook; The 100 Greatest Punchers

Ketchel came out swinging wildly at the start of the fight, and Johnson merely held him at bay with his long jab. Finally in the 12th round, Ketchel connected with a wild overhand right that caught Johnson behind the ear and dropped him to the canvas. When Johnson got up at the count of 9, Ketchel rushed in for the kill only to be met by Johnson's right hand and knocked out cold in the middle of the ring. Rumor also had it that Ketchel's front teeth were embedded in Johnson's right glove after the fight.

Ketchel took 6 months off from the ring after the Johnson fight and then fought middleweight Frank Klaus in Pittsburgh. Ketchel lost a close newspaper decision in Klaus's hometown.

Ketchel next took on the great Sam Langford in April of 1910 in Philadelphia. Ketchel and Langford fought 6 hard rounds in an even contest. A few more newspaper reporters gave the bout to Langford then to Ketchel; thus, it has been generally agreed that Langford won the newspaper decision.

Ketchel fought twice in May of 1910. He knocked out Porky Dan Flynn on May 17th in Boston and knocked out Willie Lewis in New York on May 27th.

In the last fight of his young career, Ketchel defended his middleweight title against Jim Smith in New York in June of 1910. Ketchel came out aggressively at the first bell and blasted Smith all over the ring. Ketchel finally landed a 6-punch combination to the head in the 5th round that knocked Smith out cold. This would be the last fight of Ketchel's career.

While staying at a friend's ranch house in Conway, Missouri in October of 1910 Ketchel was shot in the back by a jealous farmhand for allegedly flirting with his girlfriend.

Ketchel was generally regarded as the greatest middleweight

of all time until Sugar Ray Robinson burst on the scene in the middleweight division in the 1950's.

Ketchel's final ring record was 49 wins, 5 losses, and 3 draws with 46 wins coming by way of knockout. His knockout to win ratio is 93.9 per cent.

Ketchel was listed as the 6th greatest puncher in the 2003 Ring Magazine of the 100 greatest punchers in boxing history. He was inducted into the International Boxing Hall of Fame in 1990.

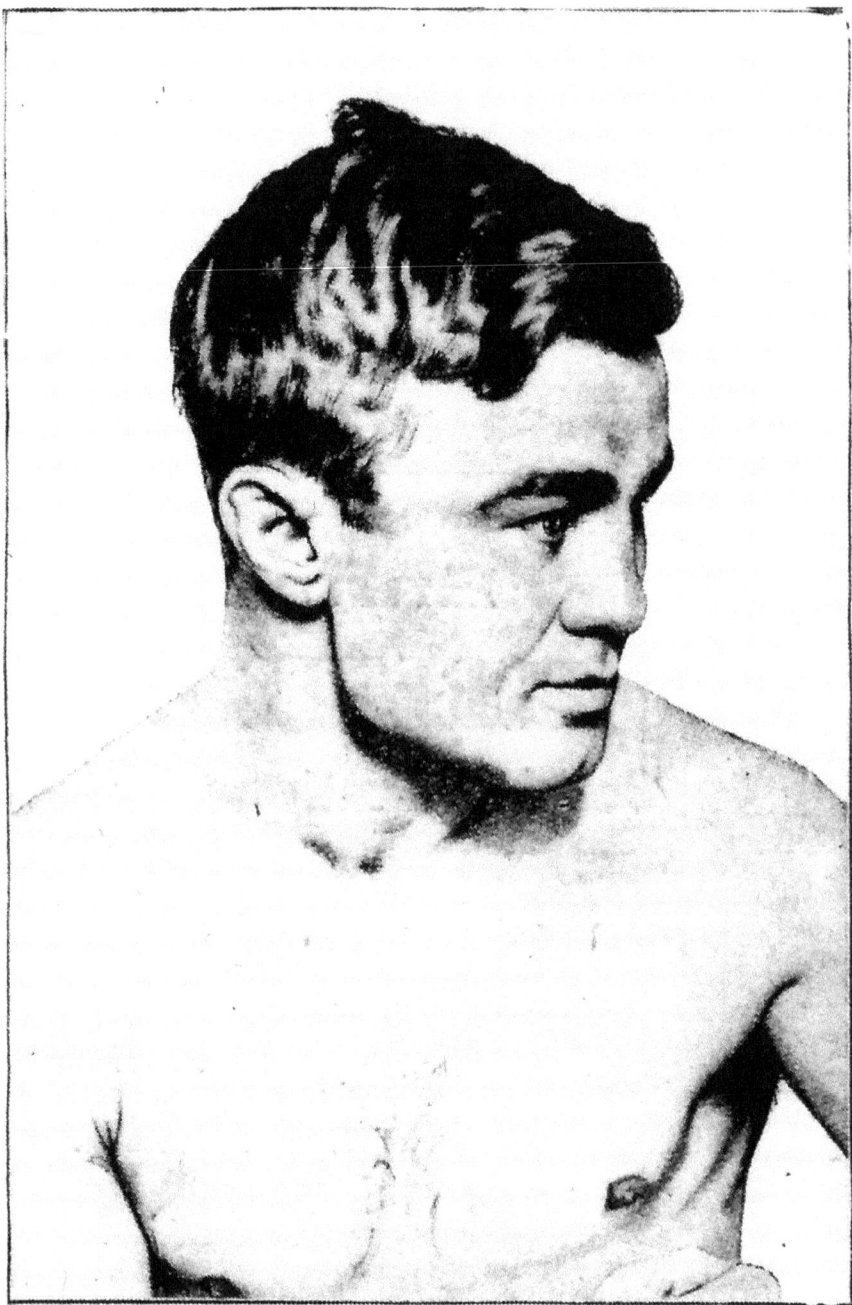

Billy Papke
The Illinois ThunderBolt, 2016

Inductee # 4 BILLY PAPKE

Billy Papke was born on September 17, 1886, in Spring Valley, Illinois, just 3 days after his future arch rival Stanley Ketchel. Papke's parents came from Germany and he worked for his parents in the livery stable business.

The only good paying jobs at the time in Spring Valley were coal mining jobs. During one of the union boycots, Papke found employment in the mines at around the age of 16.

Papke was all ready fully grown at 5'9", and weighed a very solid 155 pounds. He had broad shoulders, powerful forearms, and a small waist, giving his upper torso a v-shaped appearance.

Many of the coal miners conducted bare knuckle tough man contests where a winner was usually declared when one of the combatants was knocked unconscious and was unable to get up off of the ground. Papke just did not outbox the coal miners but he usually knocked them out cold while frequently giving away 40 to 60 pounds in weight to some opponents. Papke's reputation grew throughout Bureau County, Illinois and he was always ready to fight when he was called uncomplimentary names such as a "kraut".

Papke began frequenting local gyms and copied the style of Bantamweight and Featherweight champion Terry McGovern who usually went for the knockout as soon as the opening bell rang.

Papke's reputation as a fearsome warrior spread throughout the midwest and drew the attention of East Coast manager and promoter Tom E. Jones.

Jones saw the incredible power and stamina that Papke exhibited in his sparring sessions in Bureau County, Illinois. Jones then showed Papke how to improve his footwork and how to cut off the ring on an opponent.

While waiting to turn professional at the age of 19 he was breaking the ribs of opponents during sparring sessions with his vicious body punching and inside uppercuts.

At the age of 19, in November of 1905, Papkle made his professional debut by fighting a 6-round draw with Battling Hurley. Papke pounded Hurley at will, but a draw was declared because no knockout occurred during the contest.

Papke went undefeated in 1906 in 7 fights, winning most of his fights by knockout. Papke developed a particualry vicious short corkscrew uppercut thrown at close quarters in a fight.

On July 4th of 1906, Papke won his first 10-round main event, in LaSalle, Illinois by giving Carl Purdy a vicious beating. After registering 6 knockouts among his 7 wins, Papke quit working in the coal mines and concentrated solely on his boxing career.

Manager Tom Jones felt that he had the makings of a future champion in Papke with his incredible power in both fists and limitless stamina. In May of 1907 Papke fought his first world ranked opponent in tough Tony Caponi in Davenport, Iowa. Papke held Caponi to a draw in a brusing evenly matched 10-round fight.

Papke and Caponi fought another 10-round draw in Spring Valley, Illinois, in June of 1907. Papke ended the trilogy by knocking Caponi out in 2 rounds in November of 1907 in Peoria, Illinois. Papke was now a top ranked middleweight contender and he was promised a shot at the number one contender Hugo Kelly in the near future.

On November 22, 1907, he fought twice in Boston, Massachusetts. In his first fight he knocked out Charley Haghey in 1 round, and then returned later in the evening to knockout Bartley Connolly in 4 rounds.

On December 30, 1907, Papke held top centender Hugo Kelly to a 10-round draw in Milwaukee, Wisconsin. Papke and Kelly were signed for a rematch in March of 1908 with the winner promised a non-title fight with world middleweight champion Stanley Ketchel.

Papke and Kelly stepped into the ring at the Hippodrome in Milwaukee to do battle on March 16, 1908. On this particular night, Papke was a human punching machine as he tore into Kelly, non-stop, for the whole fight, hitting him with vicious body and head shots for the whole 10 rounds. Papke was awarded a unanimous decision in front of a cheering sold out crowd.

At this point, Papke was unbeaten in 29 fights over a 3 year period. The Ketchel vs. Papke non-title fight took place on June 4th, 1908 at the Hippodrome in Milwaukee, Wisconsin.

The bell rang for round one and when Papke came to ring center to touch gloves Ketchel reportedly tapped Papke's glove with his left hand and then drove a right cross to Papke's face. Papke landed on the seat of his pants and got up in a dazed condition. Papke fought on the defensive for the whole first round. Papke came out for the second round, not fully recovered, and took a pounding before returning to his corner with a chipped tooth.

Papke started to get back into the fight by the 3rd round, and actually dropped Ketchel to the canvas with his inside uppercut punch for a flash knockdown in the 4th round. The two warriors fought evenly for the rest of the fight. At the conclusion of the contest, the referee raised Ketchel's hand as the winner in a very competitive fight.

After the close fight, Ketchel agreed to a rematch with his title on the line if Papke would agree to a 25 round fight. Papke agreed to Ketchel's terms and the title fight was set for September 7th, 1908 in Los Angeles, California. When signing for the fight Ketchel claimed that he was not in excellent shape for their first fight, and he promised to knock Papke out in the title fight.

While getting ready for his title fight, Papke again took on 2 fighters in one night in Boston, Massachusetts, on August 13th. Papke knocked out Johnny Carroll in 2 rounds and then, later in the evening, knocked out world ranked middleweight Frank Mantell in 1 round.

Papke returned home and trained like a demon on a daily basis. Papke knew that he would probably have to knock Ketchel out to win the title and he prepared for a rugged 25-round fight.

On September 7, 1908 both gladiators stepped into the ring to do battle. Ex-heavyweight champon Jim Jeffries was the referee and he called the fighters to ring center. Jeffries gave the fighters their instructions and they returned to their respective corners.

Ketchel appeared to miss the first light punch thrown, and then it appeared he was on the canvas in a matter of moments, bleeding and dazed. Ketchel got up gamely, but Papke was all over him and dropped him to the canvas 4 more times, closing one of his eyes. Ketchel came out for round two and Papke immediately dropped him to his knees. Ketchel got up and floundered all over the ring but made it to the bell ending the 2nd round. Ketchel appeared to survive the 3rd and 4th rounds solely because Papke apparently punched himself out trying for the knockout in the first couple of rounds.

Papke gets ready to attack a bleeding and dazed Ketchel
The Illinois ThunderBolt, 2016

By the 8th round, Papke was back and landing his shots at will while Ketchel was gamely but weakly trying to make a fight of it. In the 11th round, Papke knocked Ketchel clean out of the ring, but he was able to scramble back inside the ropes before the 10-count. Papke finally ended the fight with a straight right hand to the head that dropped the exhausted and beaten Ketchel to a seated position on the canvas where he listened to the full 10-count while staring blankly at his corner.

Ketchel, back in his dressing room after the fight, claimed that he got caught off guard at the beginning of the fight and that he wanted an immediate rematch with Papke. Both of Ketchel's eyes were closed after the fight, he had suffered a broken nose, and he had amassed numerous facial cuts. Ketchel did not claim that Papke fouled him during the contest.

Papke's corner was full of jubilation and he acknowledged that he did not allow Ketchel to get the jump on him at the start of this fight, which he claimed had occurred in their Milwaukee contest.

The new champion claimed that after a short rest he would be willing to give Ketchel a rematch for the title.

Later, in the newspapers, Ketchel's cornerman Pete Stone complained that Papke hit Ketchel at the start of the contest when Ketchel went to ring center to shake hands with him. The Associated Press, however, reported that at the start of the fight Papke missed with a wild right hand and that Ketchel actually landed the first punch of the fight: a light left hand. However, it is clear that, during the first real exchange of the fight, Papke had dropped Ketchel with a left right combination to the head.

After returning home to Illinois, Papke bought a new green Stutz roadster from his earnings from the Ketchel fight.Papke had scheduled a title defense against Hugo Kelly in Milwaukee, but the week before the fight the State of Wisconsin only allowed exhibition boxing matches and not title fights.

Papke's manager, Tom Jones, advised him that he had scheduled a title defense against Ketchel on Thanksgiving Day in Calfiornia. Just days before the Ketchel fight, Papke had a dispute with his manager over his share of the purse. Needless to say, Papke entered the contest less then mentally prepared for battle.

On Thanksgiving Day in November, 1908, both fighters refused to shake hands before the contest and they walked back to their corners. Ketchel tore into Papke as soon as the match started. Ketchel would win every round of the hard fought fight and dropped his opponent flat on his back near the end of the 11th round near the ring ropes. Papke never even came close to beating the 10-count.

Papke asked Ketchel for a rematch and was advised by the champion if he could beat Hugo Kelly in a title elimination match, he would consider another match against him for the title.

In May of 1909 Papke finally proved his superiority over Kelly by cutting him up and knocking him out,to set up another title fight with Ketchel in July of 1909 in Colma, California.

Both gladiators went at each other over 20 blood-filled rounds. The fight could have been held in a telephone booth, as neither fighter gave up ground over the duration of the fight. Both fighters were covered with blood and, at the end of the contest, the referee raised Ketchel's arm as the winner by decision. The fight was close but the press agreed with the decision.

After the fight, Papke packed his bags and headed to Paris, France, in March of 1910 where he knocked out Willie Lewis in 3 rounds. Later, Papke returned to the United States and knocked out middleweight contender Joe Thomas in 16 rounds in San Francisco, California. Papke then won a 12-round decision over Jack (Twin) Sullivan in June of 1910 in Boston, Massachusetts.

October of 1910 found Papke sailing to Sydney, Australia, to fight "Big" Ed Williams when news broke that Ketchel had been shot and killed by a jealous boyfriend of a woman he had been courting in Conway, Missouri. Promoters of the match immediately billed the fight as being for the "Australian version" of the world middleweight title. Papke then proceeded to knock Williams out in the 6th round to claim the Australian version of the world middleweight title.

In February of 1911 Papke lost the Australian version of the middleweight title when he was outpointed by "Cyclone" Johnny Thompson over 20 rounds in Sydney, Australia.

In June of 1911 Papke sailed to London, England to fight Jim Sullivan for the British version of the world middleweight title. Papke stopped Sullivan in 9 rounds for the British version of the title.

In October of 1911 Thompson gave up the Australian version of the middleweight title as he was unable to make weight for the middleweight division. Papke immediately claimed the title again and sailed to Paris, France, to defend his British version of the title against Frenchman Marcel Moreau. Papke knocked out Moreau in the 16th round to claim the French version of the middleweight title.

Papke returned to Paris, France, in October of 1912, to defend his title against the popular french idol Georges Carpentier. The smooth boxing Carpentier started out fast but Papke's body blows slowed him down in the middle rounds of the fight. Carpentier sustained a huge cut over his right eye in the 17th round and was unable to come out for the bell starting the 18th round. Papke was the winner by a technical knockout. This is probably remembered as being the second most important win in his career, behind his previous knockout of Stanley Ketchel. Carpentier would later go on the win the world light heavyweight title and then challenge Jack Dempsey for the world heavyweight title.

Papke would successfully defend his title one more time when he knocked out George Bernard in Paris in 7 rounds on December 4th, 1912. Papke would lose his share of the title when he lost on a foul to Frank Klaus in Paris, in March of 1913. Papke would fight a couple of more times before he retired for good in April of 1919. Papke's legacy would be that he popularized the uppercut as a valuable in-fighting weapon as well as use of the "corkscrew punch" while fighting at close quarters.

Papke was financially secure from his ring earnings and he moved with his family to California in the 1920's. Papke bought farms, became a millionaire, and was also able to survive the Great Depression of the 1930's.

Papke made the headlines again in 1936 when he shot and killed his estranged wife before turning a gun on himself and commiting suicide. The murder-suicide made national headlines at the time.

Papke's final ring record was 37 wins, 11 losses, and 6 draws. He won 31 fights by knockout, giving him a knockout to win ratio of 83.8 per cent.

Papke was inducted in the International Boxing Hall of Fame in 2001.

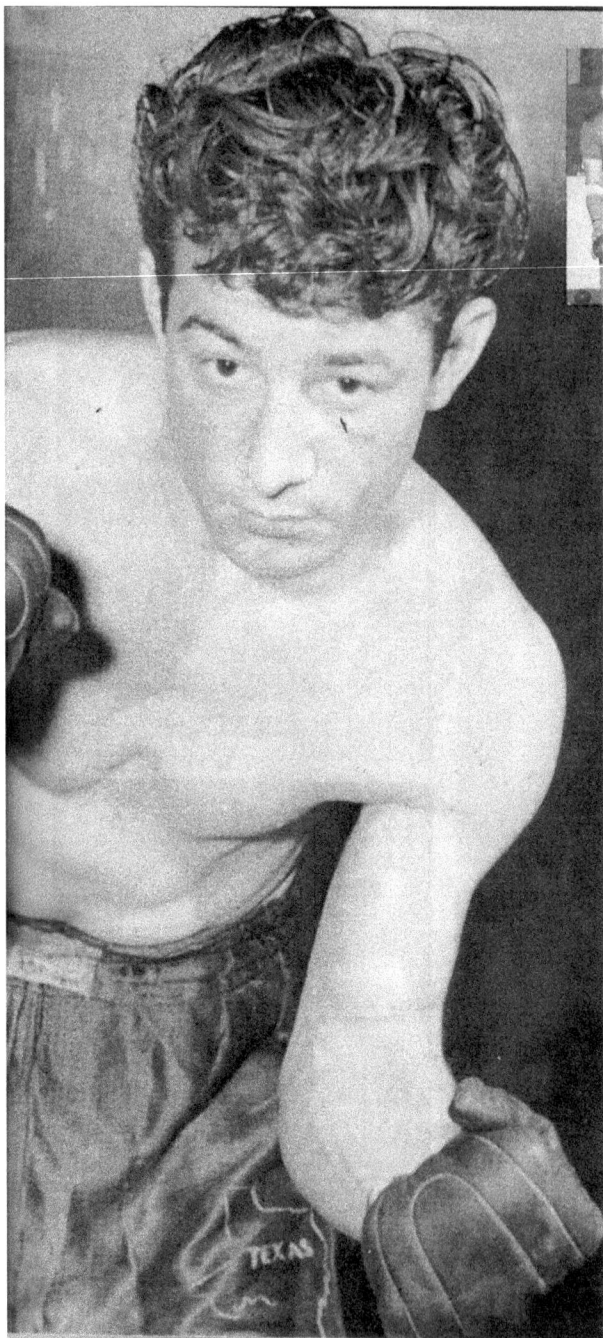

Rocky Graziano
The Ring Magazine, October 1990

Inductee # 5 ROCKY GRAZIANO

There were some excellent middleweight champions in the 1920's such as Harry Greb and Mickey Walker. The 1930's also had excellent champions such as Freddie Steele, and Al Hostak.

But none of the middleweight champions in the 1920's and 1930's had the same one-punch right hand knockout power as New York's Rocky Graziano.

Rocky Graziano was born Thomas Rocco Barbella on January 1, 1919, in New York City, New York, to Italian American parents. He spent his early years running around with New York street gangs and frequently found himself in trouble with the law for street fights and theft.

Graziano spent some time in reform schools and, after being involved in a reform school riot, was sent to the infamous Riker's Island jail. After being released from Riker's Island, he was ordered by the courts to report for military duty.

Graziano was sent to boot camp in New Jersey where, after a short stint which included punching a superior officer, he hiked back to New York City, AWOL. While back in New York City, instead of using his real name of Rocco Barbella, he used the name of a friend named Tommy Rocky Graziano to turn professional in March of 1942. He then shortened his name to Rocky Graziano to avoid detection by the military authorities.

Graziano won his first professional fight by knockout over Curtis Hightower. In his first 8 professional fights, Graziano won 5 fights, lost one fight, and had 2 draws. Graziano won all 5 of his fights by knockout.

After his 8th professional fight, with Lou Miller in May of 1942, Graziano was arrested by the military authorities for being AWOL from the Army and was sentenced to serve one year at hard labor at Fort Leavenworth, Kansas. While there, Graziano boxed on the prison's boxing team and returned to New York upon his release in May of 1943 to begin his professional career again under the management of Irving Cohen.

Graziano won his next 6 fights by knockout before he was held to a 6-round draw by Charley McPherson. Graziano had incredible power in his straight or roundhouse right hand, but he had no defense and sloppy footwork. At this point Cohen decided to hire trainer Whitey Bimstein to teach Graziano some of the finer points of boxing as he stepped up in competition.

Graziano fought 18 times in 1943 and lost just two times. Graziano was still having trouble with slick boxers who danced around the ring flicking out jabs and then getting on their bicycle. Graziano's two defeats during 1943 were to the slick boxers Steve Riggio, and Joe Acosta.

Graziano married a neighborhood girl named Norma Levine, and they celebrated the birth of their first child in May of 1944. They named their baby girl Audrey. At this point in his career, he was known as "the king of the clubs' because of his popularity in the small fight clubs in New York City. After the birth of his first child, Graziano started to get serious about his boxing and started training harder instead of just depending on the early knockout with his straight right hand.

In August of 1944 Graziano won an 8-round decision over tough Jerry Fiorello and, in October, Graziano fought to a draw with Danny Kapilow in his first 10-round fight. Graziano, later in the month knocked out Bernie Miller in 2 rounds which qualified him for his first big main event fight in Madison Square Garden against the hot young prospect Harold Green. The match with Green was set for November 3, 1944, and Green was immediately installed as the prohibitive favorite in the fight.

The promoters billed the fight as Graziano "The untamed free-swinging tiger of the clubs" versus Green "The Flatbush flattener." In the fight Green thoroughly dominated Graziano with his speed, lateral movement, and counter punching skills. Graziano did land his right hand which dropped Green to the canvas 15 seconds before the bell rang to end the fight. Green barely escaped a knockout but easily won the unanimous decision on the scorecards.

The next day the press was very critical of Graziano's overall performance and wrote that he should go back to the small fight clubs as he was definitely not a main event fighter. Graziano begged his management to get him another fight with Harold Green. Irving Cohen reluctantly agreed to try and get him a rematch due to the fact that he had nearly knocked Green out at the end of the fight.

The rematch with Green was set for December of 1944, and Green was again a huge favorite in the fight. Graziano went into serious training for this fight. Graziano put up a much better fight in the rematch but started slowly getting dropped in the 2nd round. Graziano came on strong in the second half of the fight dropping Green in the 8th round, for a 9 count, and lost a close majority decision.

Though Graziano lost his last two fights against Green, he did show enough improvement in his ring skills to be given one last shot at a Madison Square Garden main event when he was matched with local hot shot knockout artist Billy Arnold. The fight with Arnold was set for March 9, 1945, and Arnold was immediately installed as a 6-to-1 favorite in the fight. The local press wrote that Irving Cohen appeared to be trying to get Graziano killed as they felt that he was in way over his head in taking on Arnold who had a record of 29 wins, 1 loss, and 1 draw with 28 knockouts to his credit.

Graziano stepped into the ring knowing that this would probably be his last chance to get a main event victory and not have to go back to club fighting. Arnold started fast and rocked Graziano in the first two rounds. For a while it looked like it would be an easy early round knockout victory for Arnold. Graziano came out for the 3rd round swinging wildly in a desperate attempt for a knockout. Graziano stunned Arnold with a counter right hand, and then dropped him to the floor with a combination to the head. Arnold got up before the 10-count, but Graziano began pounding Arnold at will, forcing the referee to stop the fight and award him a 3rd round knockout victory. It was reported that famous reporter Damon Runyon looked at a colleague at ringside and stated, "you just witnessed the next Stanley Ketchel".

Graziano became a new type of fighter after the victory over Arnold. Graziano trained seriously and, under Whitey Bimstein's guidance, he learned to pace himself during a 10-round fight. Graziano took a tune up fight against Solomon Stewart in April of 1945 and knocked him out in 4 rounds in Washington. In May of 1945, Graziano stepped into the ring in Madison Square Garden to do battle against another puncher in Al "Bummy" Davis. The fight was an absolute brawl. Graziano came out fast and dumped Davis to the canvas in the first round. Davis returned the favor and dropped Graziano in the second round. Davis was down again twice in the third round, and Graziano put his opponent away for good in the 4th round of the wild swinging contest. Close to seventeen thousand people attended this fight and Graziano became a huge draw in the New York City area.

In June of 1945 Graziano was back in the ring in Madison Square Garden fighting world welterweight champion Freddy (Red) Cochrane in a non-title fight. Cochrane dominated the early part of the fight as Graziano stalked his opponent around the ring but could not land any serious punches. In the 9th round Graziano landed his famous right hand and Cochrane was visibly hurt. Another combination knocked Cochrane down, but he was saved by the bell. Graziano came out strong for the 10th and final round and made quick work of Cochrane. Graziano turned sure defeat into victory with his powerful right cross. The Ring magazine selected this fight as the Fight of The Year for 1945. Obviously, a rematch was in order and this fight was set for August of 1945.

The rematch with Cochrane took place in Madison Square Garden and Graziano again fell behind on the scorecards in the early going. Graziano came on strong in the late rounds and scored another technical knockout victory over Cochrane in the 10th round.

In September of 1945 Graziano settled an old score by knocking out Harold Green in New York to end their 3-fight trilogy. In March of 1946 Graziano took on welterweight champion Marty Servo in a non-title fight in Madison Square Garden.

Graziano appeared much larger than Servo in the ring, and the welterweight champion was no match for Graziano. Graziano busted up Servo badly in the second round, breaking his nose and knocking him out. Servo retired temporarily after this crushing defeat and gave up his welterweight title.

Graziano was now the number 1 contender for Tony Zale's middleweight title. The title fight was set for September of 1946 in New York's Madison Square Garden. Zale had been champion since 1940 and he was a rugged, strong, body-punching type of fighter.

Graziano started strong in the title fight dropping Zale in the early rounds and staggering him in the 3rd round. Zale started to come back in the 4th round by going to Graziano's body. Zale was behind on the scorecards and battered when he hurt Graziano with a body punch in the 6th round, and then dropped him with a hook. Graziano failed to beat the 10-count and Zale won a come-from-behind 6th round knockout. The exciting fight called for a rematch, but it would not be held in New York.

It was reported that Graziano did not report a bribe that was made to him to throw a fight, against Ruben Shank and the New York State Athletic Commission suspended his boxing license in 1947. History shows there was never any proof that Graziano ever threw a fight. The return match with Zale was then set for Chicago Stadium in Illinois for July of 1947. The National Boxing Association sanctioned the title fight and did not go along with the New York State suspension.

In the rematch, Zale came out in the first round looking for a knockout, and Graziano came back to his corner at the end of the round with a badly cut left eye. Zale went after Graziano's cut eye in the second round and continued to hammer away at his ribs. Zale dropped Graziano for a short count before the 2nd round ended. Graziano took a beating in the 3rd round, and his left eye began to close. The referee came to his corner at the end of the round and threatened to stop the fight if he did not do better in the next round.

Graziano came out for the 4th round with his left eye closed, and began fighting like a street fighter, throwing wild left hooks, and overhand rights in non-stop fashion. The tempo of the fight escalated in the 5th round, with both fighters staggering each other. Graziano hurt Zale in ring center in the 6th round, with a right hand and followed him to the ropes where he poured nonstop leather on Zale until he had laid him helpless across the top of the ring ropes. Zale was unable to stand or fight back, and the referee stopped the battle and awarded the fight and the middleweight title to Graziano.

Graziano, the New York bad boy, had finally made it to the top of the middleweight division. Graziano then won a couple of tune up fights, but since his New York license was still under suspension, the rubber match with Zale would be held in Newark, New Jersey in June of 1948.

Graziano knocking out Tony Zale for the middleweight title
Boxing International All-Star Wrestling, July 1965

Graziano was dropped in the first round of the rubber match, but he tried to fight back in the second round. Graziano was knocked out in the 3rd round by a picture-perfect left hook, that knocked him flat on his back with his head bouncing off of the canvas when he hit the ring floor.

Graziano returned to the ring in 1949 and won all 4 of his fights with 3 coming by knockout. Graziano was undefeated in his 9 fights in 1950, including a 10-round draw, and then a 10-round decision win over arch middleweight rival Tony Janiro. Graziano won all 6 of his fights in 1951 including a TKO victory over Tony Janiro in their rubber match.

Graziano won a couple of tune up fights in 1952 and then challenged champion Sugar Ray Robinson for the middleweight title in April of 1952 in Chicago Stadium. Graziano dropped Robinson in the 3rd round with a right hand to the side of the head, but Robinson came back later in the round to drop and stop his opponent.

Graziano retired after losing a televised 10-round decision to contender Chuck Davey in September of 1952 in Chicago Stadium.

After retirement Graziano made regular television appearances on the Martha Raye Television Show and wrote an autobiography with Rowland Barber titled "Somebody Up There Likes Me" in 1955. In 1956 his book led to a movie of the same name starring Paul Newman, and Pier Angeli.

Graziano was a pure slugger in the ring, and it has been said that his straight right hand was one of the deadliest punches ever thrown in the middleweight division. Graziano was also one of the most popular ring champions of all time.

Graziano passed away in 1990 at the age of 71 His final ring record was 67 wins, 10 losses, and 6 draws. He won 52 fights by knockout. His knockout to win percentage was 77.6 per cent.

The 2003 edition of Ring magazine lists Graziano as the 23rd greatest puncher of all time. Graziano was inducted into the International Boxing Hall of Fame in 1991.

Eduardo Lausse
Boxing Illustrated. June 1960

Inductee # 6 EDUARDO LAUSSE

When Argentine middleweight champion Carlos Monzon came to New York to fight middleweight contender Tony Licata in June of 1975 he was asked if he thought that Sugar Ray Robinson was the greatest middleweight champion in history. Monzon was also asked how he thought he would have fared in a fight against Robinson, and if Robinson was his hero growing up in Argentina.

Monzon simply replied that he did not know much about Robinson, and that his hero growing up was Argentine middleweight Eduardo Lausse who had fought back in the 1950's and was the South American middleweight champion. Monzon further stated that many of the amateur tournaments in Buenos Aires were named after Lausse.

So, who was Eduardo Lausse? Eduardo Lausse was born on November 27th, 1927, in the Lomas de Zamora section of Buenos Aires, Argentina. He was a strong, sturdily built youth and he turned professional as a welterweight in the famed Luna Park Stadium in Buenos Aires in March of 1947 by knocking out Jorge McCaddon.

Lausse was a converted southpaw and he had developed tremendous power in his left hook. Prior to turning professional, Lausse had signed a contract to be managed by local fight figure Tino Porzio.

Lausse became an immediate sensation with the Luna Park fight crowd as he won his first 17 professional fights with 15 wins coming by knockout. The local boxing aficionados were starting to compare Lausse with the current middleweight champion at that time Rocky Graziano and with former Argentine heavyweight contender Luis Firpo. In December of 1947 Lausse's management team felt that he was ready take on the more experienced Argentine welterweight champion Amelio Piceda.

Piceda was a veteran of over 60 professional fights, and he was just too experienced for the young Argentine power puncher. Lausse had his moments in the fight when he rocked Picedo with left hooks, but the cagey veteran knew how to box his way out of trouble.

Lausse was back into the ring in March of 1948 when he won a 10-round decision over Kid Cachetada. In May Lausse knocked out Julio Fiardina and Antonio Pangaro in August.

In September of 1948 Lausse received another lesson in the finer points of boxing when he lost a decision to Mario Diaz. Diaz was another veteran of over 50 fights to his credit

Lausse went on an 8 fight unbeaten streak, before he lost 10 round decisions in return matches with Kid Cachetada and Mario Diaz in 1950.

Lausse won his next 4 fights before he was surprised and stopped by Antonio Cuevas in April of 1952. In September of 1952 world welterweight champion Kid Gavilan was touring South America and looking for opponents in non-title bouts. Lausse was selected to be his first opponent on the tour, and the local press was criticizing his management for continually putting their young tiger in with more experienced opponents.

Lausse surprised the boxing experts, and Kid Gavilan, by giving an excellent account of himself in losing a close 10-round decision to the champion. Lausse severely rocked Gavilan on several occasions during the fight.

After the Gavilan fight, Lausse went on a 7-fight winning streak, with 6 of the wins coming by knockout. Lausse had outgrown the welterweight division and the move up to the middleweight division seemed to increase his punching power.

American fight manager Charley Johnston was touring South America with light heavyweight champion Archie Moore when he heard about Lausse's vaunted punching power. Johnston saw Lausse work out, and he was so impressed with his left hook and raw power that he immediately signed him to a series of fights in the United States.

Lausse had his first fight in the United States in February of 1953 when he knocked out Johnny Darby in White Plains, New York. Lausse returned to the same ring in March and knocked out Gus Mell. In April, Lausse was brought to Providence, Rhode Island and knocked out Tommy Smith.

After Lausse's short successful fight tour of the United States, he immediately returned home to Argentina as he had become homesick. Lausse's frequent trips back to Argentina throughout his life would become a frequent source of agitation to Charley Johnston, as he felt that it was disrupting the progress Lausse was making in his career in the United States.

In May of 1953, back home in Argentina, Lausse knocked out Antonio Frontado, and in June Lausse knocked out Antonio Cuevas in an impressive rematch.

In July of 1953 Lausse won the vacant Argentine version of the middleweight title when he knocked out Mario Diaz in their rubber match. Lausse continued on his winning streak by winning 7 more fights in Argentina all by knockout before Charley Johnston could talk him into returning to the United States for another tour of fighting the top contenders in the middleweight division.

Lausse returned to fight in the United States in April of 1954 after having won his last 19 fights by knockout. Lausse took on cagey veteran Jesse Turner and was lucky to win a split decision from the veteran in Eastern Parkway Arena, in Brooklyn, New York. In May Lausse fought at the St. Nicks Arena in New York and demolished veteran Chico Varona. Charley Johnston now felt that Lausse was ready to debut at Madison Square Garden and he was matched with veteran Joe Rindone at that venue in June of 1954. The New York fight crowd was very impressed with how Lausse knocked out Rindone easily in just a couple of rounds. Lausse's left hook power reminded some of the veteran reporters of the power that Rocky Graziano had in his right hand a decade previously.

Unfortunately, Lausse was back on a plane again to Argentina where he won 5 fights by knockout to close out 1954. Charley Johnston promised to get Lausse fights with top middleweight contenders, and he returned to the United States in March of 1955 to defeat Gil Edwards in Providence, Rhode Island. In April he knocked Georgie Small out cold in Boston, Massachusetts.

In May of 1955 Lausse returned to Madison Square Garden in New York City to fight the main event against world ranked middleweight contender Ralph "Tiger" Jones. Jones had impressively and surprisingly beaten former champion Sugar Ray Robinson in his comeback to the ring.

In a brutal and bloody ring war, Lausse pounded out a 10 round unanimous decision victory over the very rugged and durable Jones. Unfortunately, Lausse suffered severe facial injuries in the contest and, as usual, he returned to Argentina for his next big fight.

In September of 1955 he took on Kid Gavilan, the now ex-welterweight champion of the world, in a rematch. Lausse had improved greatly since their first match with a bob and weave type of defense and tuck and roll style of avoiding punches as is seen in modern boxers today in the likes of Floyd Mayweather Junior. Lausse was very impressive in winning a 12-round decision over Gavilan, and he was now up high in the top 10 middleweight world ratings.

In October of 1955 Lausse knocked out Oscar Barreiro in Montevideo, Uruguay, to earn a middleweight title elimination match against Gene Fullmer in New York in November of 1955.

Charley Johnston began negotiating behind the scenes for a title shot against champion Carl "Bobo" Olson if Lausse defeated Fullmer. Apparently, a sticking point was that the Porzio clan in Argentina were reluctant to give the champion options in the contract if Olson lost.

Lausse drops and defeats future middleweight champion
Gene Fullmer
Boxing Illustrated, June 1960

In November of 1955 Lausse stepped into the ring to do battle with Fullmer in New York. Both fighters were known to be aggressive sluggers who rarely took a backward step.

The fight began and it was obvious from the start that Lausse was the physically stronger of the two fighters as Fullmer fought cautiously due to the power in Lausse's left hook. Lausse would press forward and Fullmer would jump in and counter punch and then back out of the fray from a safe distance. Lausse built up a lead in the early rounds and dropped Fullmer for a flash knockdown in the 8th round. Fullmer fought back hard to the end of the fight, but the judges awarded Lausse a well-earned unanimous decision.

Unfortunately for Lausse, by this time Olson had signed instead to defend his title against Sugar Ray Robinson in December in Chicago. Lausse correctly stated after the Fullmer fight, that he felt that Robinson would beat Olson for the title, and then would never give him a title fight.

Lausse stayed busy and knocked out Johnny Sullivan in spectacular fashion in Cleveland, Ohio, in December of 1955. In February of 1956 Lausse took on another top middleweight contender in Bobby Boyd in his hometown of Chicago.

The fight was rough from the start and Lausse received a severe cut between the eyes from a head butt which hampered him during the fight. Lausse did drop Boyd once during the fight, but the two battlers fought evenly for the rest of the fight. Boyd was awarded a split decision victory which angered Lausse and his manager Charley Johnston. Lausse felt that he had won the fight, and Johnston claimed that the severe cut from the head butt cost Lausse 2 rounds of the fight.

Despondent, Lausse returned again to Argentina where he gained the South American middleweight title in June of 1956 by knocking out Humberto Loayza in Buenos Aires. Lausse would then defend his title by knocking out Luis Colman in General Martin, Argentina, in August of 1956. Lausse would eventually lose his South American title to Andres Selpa by technical knockout in October of 1956.

Lausse ended up knocking out Antonio Cuevas in their rubber match in October of 1957, and then won a decision over Andres Selpa in 1958 to end their 3-fight trilogy.

In 1959, the middleweight division had two recognized title holders. Gene Fullmer was recognized as middleweight champion by the National Boxing Association, and Paul Pender was recognized as champion in New York, and Massachusetts.

Charley Johnston advised Lausse that if he returned to the United States and fought a couple of times, that he felt he could get one of the two champions into the ring to defend their title against him.

Lausse returned to New York in June of 1959 and looked impressive in knocking out the tough Canadian contender Wilfie Greaves.

In Lausse's last hurdle before taking on one of the two middleweight champions, he took on tough Frenchman Marcel Pigou in New York.

Lausse started the fight strong, and Pigou was saved by the bell ending the 5th round. At that point, it appeared referee Arthur Mercante appeared ready to stop the fight. Pigou recovered and it appeared Lausse may have punched himself out by the 6th round in trying for the 5th round knockout. Pigou dropped Lausse for a knockdown in the 7th round, and while it appeared he was bobbing and weaving under Pigou's desperate attempt at a knockout, referee Mercante jumped in and stopped the fight. Pigou was awarded a technical knockout victory with Lausse way ahead on the scorecards.

It appeared that Pigou was in far worse shape at the end of the 5th round, then Lausse was in the 7th round. Lausse then left a fighting career in the United States for good. Lausse fought one last time in March of 1960 in Argentina, winning by knockout, and then permanently retired from the sport.

Lausse came close to earning a title fight, but luck was not with him. Lausse's frequent trips back to Argentina did not endear him to United States boxing promoters and in 1955, and 1956, the only middleweight title fights were between Sugar Ray Robinson, and Bobo Olson. If it is true that his management in Argentina hindered his chances at getting a title shot, that could be another cause for him not getting a title fight as he certainly did not lack the ability to be a strong contender.

In the 1950's there was just one middleweight boxing champion and boxing was controlled by the International Boxing Club's James D. Norris, who worked out of Chicago. The International Boxing Club was eventually broken up by the government as a monopoly.

In today's world of 2 or 3 different middleweight champions, it would almost be a certainty that Lausse would hold at least one of the belts. Most ring historians also believe that Lausse would have had a good chance of knocking out Bobo Olson if he had received that title fight at the end of 1955.

In retirement Lausse opened up a gym, appliance store, pizza parlor, and motorcycle shop. Lausse was a fighter who possessed the best left hook in the division during the 1950's and he had the stamina to knock an opponent out early, or late, in a fight. Lausse was also underrated as a defensive fighter. There are videos on You Tube that show him slipping and sliding underneath punches along with ones showing him rolling his shoulders to avoid direct punches as many fighters do to this day.

Lausse remained a very popular figure in Argentina all the way up until his death in 1994 at the age of 66. He was known in his home country as "el campeon sin corona" the champion without a crown.

Lausse's final ring record was 75 wins, 10 losses, and 2 draws. He won 62 fights by knockout for a knockout to win ratio of 82.7 per cent.

In the 2003 Ring Magazine, Lausse was rated as the 84th greatest puncher in boxing history.

Florentino Fernandez
Ring News by Eric Armitt

Inductee # 7 *FLORENTINO FERNANDEZ*

If Eduardo Lausse had the best left hook in the middleweight division in the 1950's, then Cuba's Florentino Fernandez certainly had the best left hook in the division in the 1960's.

Florentino (Ox) Fernandez was born on March 7, 1936, in Santiago de Cuba. His strength was evident when, while a young boy, he would get into street fights and knockout all of the other young boys.

As an amateur he won 18 of 20 bouts, including a win over future welterweight champion Luis Rodriguez in a Cuban golden gloves match.

Fernandez who was a natural southpaw, was converted to an orthodox stance while still in the amateurs. His supernatural power was evident even in his first few amateur matches.

The powerful Fernandez turned professional in 1956 at the age of 20, and was undefeated in his first 21 fights, winning 18 fights by knockout. Among his first 21 fights, his first big name opponent was welterweight contender Rocky Randall. Fernandez knocked Randall out with ease in October of 1958.

In May of 1959 Fernandez fought former world lightweight champion Paddy DeMarco and knocked him out in Havana, Cuba. All of Fernandez's fights had been in Havana, Cuba, and his impressive string of knockouts earned him a fight in Madison Square Garden in New York City against veteran Stefan Redl in June of 1959. The fight with Redl was televised nationally throughout the United States. Redl had gone the distance with top contenders and had never been stopped in his career.

Fernandez knocks out Stefan Redl on national television
The Ring Magazine September 1998

Fernandez started out the fight aggressively jabbing and hooking, but not really hurting Redl. Finally, in the 7th round, Fernandez landed his left hook and down went Redl on the seat of his pants. Redl did beat the 10-count but, once he was up, he was unable to continue the fight.

The New York fight crowd saw that Fernandez had power in his left fist, but at times he appeared a bit amateurish when trying to set up an opponent for the knockout.

In September of 1959, Fernandez fought his first ranked welterweight in Gasper "Indian" Ortega. Ortega had 68 professional fights and had a top 10 ranking in the welterweight division. The fight was held in Miami Beach, Florida.

Fernandez came out of his corner flashing his left hook and Ortega was down in the first round. Fernandez was wild with his follow up punches and Ortega survived the round. Fernandez caught Ortega with his left hook again and dropped Ortega in the fourth round. Ortega got up and got on his bicycle for the remainder of the fight. Fernandez was given a unanimous decision win over the 6th ranked welterweight contender.

Ortega asked for a rematch, and this fight took place in October of 1959 at Madison Square Garden in New York City.

Ortega fought from a distance in the rematch, and made Fernandez look bad at times. Fernandez, however, did just enough in the ring to win a split decision over the wily veteran.

In November of 1959 Fernandez traveled to Caracas, Venezuela to take on another rated fighter named Rocky Kalingo from the Philippines. Kalingo caught Fernandez cold in the 1st round and stopped him. This snapped his unbeaten streak of 24 fights.

Fernandez got Kalingo back inside the ring in his hometown of Havana, Cuba, in December of 1959, and reversed his only loss by stopping Kalingo in the 2nd round.

The Kalingo loss set Fernandez back a bit as he continued to pursue the world title. In March of 1960 Fernandez traveled to Miami Beach, Florida and took on world ranked welterweight contender

Ralph Dupas. Dupas was known as a real "cutie" in the ring and used the "New Orleans" style of sticking and moving to avoid punches.

Fernandez solved Dupas style of boxing by pressing the action and fighting inside. Fernandez took the decision over Dupas and followed up that big win by knocking out Gerald Grey in Havana, Cuba, in April of 1960.

Fernandez was back in Madison Square Garden in August of 1960 fighting another future rising star in Emile Griffith of the Virgin Islands. Fernandez was having a hard time fighting at the welterweight limit of 147 pounds and he appeared sluggish in the ring, chasing Griffith and losing a 10-round decision.

In November of 1960 Fernandez moved up to the 160-pound middleweight division, and he knocked out Phil Moyer in 5 rounds in Madison Square Garden. It was obvious that Fernandez still had his power in the heavier division, and this meant he did not have to lose up to 10 pounds just before a fight to make the division weight limit.

Fernandez returned to the ring in January of 1961 to knock out middleweight contender Rory Calhoun in 8 rounds in Madison Square Garden. This win led to a middleweight title elimination match with rugged Frenchman Marcel Pigou in March of 1961. Fernandez blasted out Pigou in 2 rounds and then challenged middleweight champion Gene Fullmer for title.

The title match against Fullmer was set for August 5, 1961, in Ogden, Utah. Fullmer liked to defend his title close to his home state and this title defense would be no different.

Fullmer won most of the early rounds by smothering Fernandez's attack through fighting on the inside and not giving him room to punch. Fernandez then picked up the attack and matched

Fullmer's body attack, punch for punch, during the inside fighting, and took rounds 5 through 8.

Fernandez started to come on strong after the 12th round, but Fullmer had built up a big early lead over him. By the 14th round Fullmer was tiring and Fernandez switched to a southpaw attack. Fullmer became confused as Fernandez hammered away at him in the 14th, and 15th rounds. Fullmer was barely able to last the distance, but he took all of Fernandez's punishment without going down. The scoring was close, but Fullmer was awarded a split decision victory by the judges. It was revealed after the fight that one of Fernandez's punches broke a bone in Fullmer's right elbow, and he had fought the last round one armed. Fullmer refused to give Fernandez a rematch and this would be Fernandez's only title fight in his boxing career.

Fernandez returned to the ring in January of 1962 to re-establish his career. Fernandez took on fellow contender Dick Tiger from Nigeria in Miami Beach, Florida, in January of 1962. Fernandez was battling Tiger on even terms until a counter right hand broke his nose and the fight had to be stopped due to the excessive bleeding. The fight was awarded to Tiger.

In April of 1962 Fernandez returned to Miami Beach to take on veteran contender Joey Giambra. Giamba opened up a cut over old scar tissue over one of Fernandez's eyes, and Giambra continued to work on the cut until the fight was stopped in his favor by an 8th round technical knockout.

Fernandez had now lost 3 fights in a row and some of the ring experts wondered if his career was over. Fernandez answered that question, by returning to the ring in August of 1962, and knocking out old foe Phil Moyer in 7 rounds in Moyer's hometown of Eugene, Oregon.

In October of 1962 Fernandez returned to Madison Square Garden to take on fellow knockout artist Rubin "Hurricane" Carter. The Carter fight would be determined by which fighter could land their knockout punch first.

Carter beat Fernandez to the punch with a counter right hand in the first round which dropped him in the center of the ring. Fernandez got up immediately but then Carter followed him to the ring ropes and blasted him with a left hook and right cross to the head which knocked him through the ring ropes and out cold on the ring apron. The photo of Carter snarling and bent over Fernandez as he was tangled in the ropes was a popular photo at the time in all the boxing magazines.

Three months later Fernandez bounced back again by knocking out contender Hilario Morales in Jacksonville, Florida, and then traveled to San Juan, Puerto Rico, to knock out local favorite Obdulio Nunez in February of 1963.

The Nunez victory set up a showdown with unbeaten Puerto Rican sensation Jose Torres in May of 1963. Torres was unbeaten in 27 fights and was a powerful body puncher. In later years he would go on to become the world light heavyweight champion.

The Torres fight would be Fernandez's finest hour in his ring career. For 4 rounds Fernandez and Torres took turns staggering each other with vicious combinations to the head and body. The action was toe to toe, with neither fighter backing up. Finally in the 5th round, Fernandez broke through with vicious left hooks to the body that took Torres' legs away from him. Torres went down on the canvas twice from combinations. Fernandez continued to batter Torres when he got up the second time on shaky legs, and the referee stopped the fight and awarded the victory to Fernandez. This was the biggest win of Fernandez's career.

After the fight, the Puerto Rican fans stood up and cheered both fighters and invited Fernandez back to Puerto Rico again to fight.

In August of 1963 Fernandez returned to San Juan, Puerto Rico again and knocked out American Randy Sandy. In October of 1963 Fernandez traveled to Boston, Massachusetts, to knock out local fighter Joey DeNucci.

In November of 1963 Fernandez returned to Madison Square Garden and lost a unanimous decision to fellow middleweight puncher Rocky Rivero from Argentina. Rivero was a rough and tumble fighter like Fernandez, and he scored an 8th round knockdown in the fight.

In December of 1963 the two warriors fought again, and Fernandez won on a 7th round technical knockout when the fight had to be stopped due to a severe cut over one of Rivero's eyes.

In February of 1964 Fernandez and Rivero met for a 3rd time in San Juan, Puerto Rico. Fernandez won a unanimous decision over Rivero in a 10-round all-action nonstop war.

By 1965 Fernandez had past his peak and was starting to slow down in the ring as he went on a 5-fight losing streak, losing to the likes of Jose Gonzales, Jimmy Lester, Andy Heilman, Carl Moore, and his old foe, Rocky Rivero.

In 1967 Fernandez won and lost fights to Willie Tiger by knockout, and then retired after getting knocked out by Luis Gutierrez in Miami in April.

In 1969 Fernandez made a comeback as a light heavyweight and still maintained his punch even as he had slowed down inside of the ring.

Fernandez knocked out Lou Howard in October of 1969 and drew with Joe Aska in January of 1970 in Coconut Grove, Florida.

Fernandez then went on a 6-fight winning streak as he made a run for the light heavyweight title. A knockout loss to Vernon McIntosh in July of 1972 ended his light heavyweight title hopes, and his ring career.

Fernandez lived in Florida after his ring retirement and worked as a recreational counselor and boxing instructor for Dade County.

Fernandez had a fine career, but he regretted the fact that he never got a return match with Gene Fullmer for the title and was unable to reap the rewards of being a champion.

Fernandez's final ring record was 50 wins, 16 losses, and 1 draw. He won 43 fights by knockout, for a knockout to win ratio of 86 per cent.

The 2003 Ring Magazine edition listed Fernandez as the 56th greatest puncher of all time.

Fernandez died in January of 2013 in Miami, Florida at the age of 76.

Bennie Briscoe
The Ring Magazine 2003 Yearbook; The 100 Greatest Punchers

Inductee # 8 BENNIE BRISCOE

The man known as "Bad" Bennie Briscoe was born in Augusta, Georgia, on February 8, 1943, to a very poor family as one of fourteen children.

At the young age of 16, Briscoe moved to Philadelphia, Pennsylvania, to live with an aunt. While in Philadelphia, he began training alongside heavyweight Joe Frazier. Briscoe, due to his many training sessions with Frazier, picked up his bobbing and weaving along with his aggressive style of fighting.

While in Philadelphia, Briscoe picked up employment with the city's sanitation department, and sent part of his earned money to help out his family in Georgia.

As an amateur, Briscoe compiled a record of 70 wins with only 3 losses. Briscoe won the local Amateur Athletic Union title 3 times but never made it to the Olympic trials because of his professional style of in fighting.

Briscoe turned professional at the age of 19 in September of 1962 by winning a decision over Sam Samuels in Philadelphia. Under trainer Quenzell McCall, Briscoe won his first 15 professional fights, with 10 of his wins coming by knockout. His most impressive victories were a 1 round knockout of Charley Scott for the Pennsylvania welterweight title in March of 1964, and an 8th round technical knockout over Percy Manning in June of 1964.

Briscoe lost his first fight in a rematch with Percy Manning by a close split decision in March of 1965 in Philadelphia. The fight was close but Manning managed to stay one step ahead of the plodding Briscoe for most of the fight.

Briscoe rebounded with 2 impressive wins and then fought top ten welterweight contender Stanley "Kitten" Hayward in December of 1965 in Philadelphia. In a torrid slugfest Hayward edged out Briscoe by split decision.

Briscoe knocked out C.L. Lewis, and then fought another Philadelphia legend George Benton in December of 1966. After taking a systematic beating, Benton was unable to come off of his stool for the 10th and final round. In this battle, Briscoe gained his most impressive victory to date.

In March of 1967 Briscoe fought former world welterweight champion Luis Rodriguez from Cuba in Philadelphia. Rodriguez proved too experienced for the aggressive Briscoe and won a well-deserved unanimous decision.

In May of 1967 Briscoe traveled to Buenos Aires, Argentina to fight future middleweight champion Carlos Monzon.

In a rough and tumble 10-round war, Briscoe earned a draw with the future champion. Briscoe later stated that earning a draw against Monzon in Argentina would have been like a win in any other country. The two fighters would meet again in the future.

Briscoe returned home to Philadelphia and took his next 4 fights by knockout before he lost a rematch with Luis Rodriguez by unanimous decision again in December of 1967. Elusive boxers would always remain a problem for Briscoe throughout his entire ring career.

In August of 1968 Briscoe knocked out Gene "Honeybear" Bryant in Las Vegas in 8 rounds and then, just 2 weeks later, won a unanimous 10-round decision over Jose Gonzalez in Madison Square Garden in New York City.

Now fighting as a middleweight, Briscoe traveled to San Juan, Puerto Rico, and lost a decision to future light heavyweight champion Vicente Rondon in September of 1968. In January of 1969 Briscoe returned to San Juan, Puerto Rico, and knocked out Rondon in a return match.

In February of 1969 Briscoe lost a close split decision to slick boxer Juarez de Lima at the Felt Forum in New York City.

Briscoe returned to Madison Square Garden in March of 1969 and knocked out Jose Gonzalez in a rematch in 5 rounds. In May of 1969 Briscoe would win his rubber match with Percy Manning by a 4th round knockout in Philadelphia.

In September of 1969 the inconsistent Briscoe would lose an upset 10-round majority decision to underdog Joe "Buzzsaw" Shaw at the Spectrum in Philadelphia.

In March of 1970 Briscoe would knock out Shaw in 7 rounds in a rematch in Philadelphia, and this would be the start of a 2 year, 11 fight unbeaten streak for him. On the verge of a title shot at now world middleweight champion, Carlos Monzon, Briscoe would unexpectedly lose a split 10-round decision to the unknown Luis Vinales in Scranton, Pennsylvania, in April of 1972. Luckily for Briscoe he was able to entice Vinales back into the ring in Philadelphia in October of 1972. Briscoe made sure he did not let the rematch depend upon the judges' decision, and he stopped Vinales in 7 rounds. Briscoe would now challenge Monzon for the world title in Buenos Aires in November of 1972.

The title fight started with Briscoe, as usual, plodding after the counter punching champion who was piling up the points with his jab and straight right hand. Finally in the 9th round Briscoe stunned Monzon near the ropes with a perfect right hand to the jaw. Monzon froze in his tracks and held onto the ring ropes to remain upright. Briscoe hesitated in his attack and let Monzon off of the hook before the round ended. Monzon would continue to pile up the points with his superior boxing and rocked Briscoe with combinations in the 13th round. Briscoe could just not get past Monzon's jab on a consistent basis and Monzon coasted to a well-earned unanimous decision victory. Briscoe, in March of 1973, knocked out Art Hernandez in 3 rounds in Philadelphia to claim the North American Boxing Federation middleweight title. In June of 1973 he would defend the title successfully by stopping Billy "Dynamite" Douglas in 8 rounds.

Briscoe defeats Billy Douglas
The Ring Magazine 2003 Yearbook; The 100 Greatest Punchers

In September of 1973 Briscoe traveled to Noumea, Caledonia, and lost a unanimous decision to the top Colombian middleweight contender Rodrigo Valdes.

In February of 1974 Briscoe traveled to Paris, France, to fight the number 1 middleweight contender Tony Mundine from Australia. Mundine was being groomed for a title fight against Carlos Monzon and he regarded the Briscoe fight as a tune up for his upcoming title fight. Mundine had recently decisioned former middleweight champion Emile Griffith. Mundine had success against Griffith because he had boxed him from a distance.

Mundine was unable to keep Briscoe off of him as Briscoe kept plodding forward behind a thudding left jab followed by left hooks and right crosses. Briscoe cornered Mundine in the 5th round and knocked him down before the referee counted him out and awarded the fight to Briscoe in a mild upset. The Mundine victory may have been one of Briscoe's finest fights where he, at last, put all his ring skills together.

In the Spring of 1974, the World Boxing Council stripped Monzon of his middleweight title for not defending his title against their number 1 contender, Rodrigo Valdes. Briscoe was named to oppose Valdes in a rematch for the title in May of 1974 in Monte Carlo.

Valdes started off strong in the rematch by staggering Briscoe in the first round. Valdes was doing well in the fight until he suffered a cut eye in the 4th round. Briscoe began to pick up the pace and by the 7th round he had started to take control of the fight. Briscoe was on the attack when Valdes caught him with a right hand and left hook which put Briscoe on the seat of his pants. Briscoe got up before the 10-count, but his legs were unstable, and the referee stopped the fight and awarded the match and the vacant title to Valdes. This was the only fight in Briscoe's ring career where he would be stopped.

Briscoe returned to The Spectrum in Philadelphia in October of 1974 to take on former middleweight champion Emile Griffith. Griffith had enough talent left to outhustle Briscoe over 10 rounds to win a majority decision.

In June of 1975 Briscoe won a unanimous decision over Stanley "Kitten' Hayward in a rematch and, in August of 1975, Briscoe won a 10-round split decision over the future light heavyweight champion Eddie Mustapha Muhammed in Philadelphia.

In November of 1975 Briscoe took on fellow Philadelphia middleweight slugger Eugene "Cyclone" Hart at the Spectrum in Philadelphia. Both sluggers fought a non-stop 10-round war. Neither fighter ever gave ground in the fight and Hart would later claim that it was the greatest fight that he had ever fought; he also felt that he deserved the decision instead of a draw.

In April of 1976 Briscoe and Hart would fight again for bragging rights as to who was the top dog puncher in the Philadelphia area. As sometimes happens when two sluggers meet, one will catch the other cold in the first round as when Rubin Carter caught Florentino Fernandez cold in the first round in 1962. This time around it was no contest, as Briscoe caught Hart cold in the 1st round and knocked him out.

In June of 1976 Briscoe took on Emile Griffith in a rematch and the best he could do was a dubious draw. Briscoe then went on a 5-fight winning streak which included knockouts over name opponents Jean Mateo and Sammy Barr.

By 1977 Carlos Monzon had defeated Rodrigo Valdes twice to unify the title before retiring. The world middleweight title was now at stake and old foes Rodrigo Valdes and Briscoe were matched, once again, for all the belts.

The title fight was held in November of 1977 in Campione d' Italia. As usual, Valdes started off strong with his combination punching, but Briscoe started to come on in the middle rounds, and even knocked Valdes' mouthpiece out in the 12th round. Valdes then outhustled Briscoe in the last 3 rounds to win a unanimous decision and the vacant title.

Briscoe was bitter after the fight and claimed that he was robbed of the decision by the officials. It seemed like Briscoe knew that this would be his last chance to win a title, and it had just slipped out of his fingers. Other than Briscoe's trainer George Benton, most boxing officials agreed with the verdict.

Briscoe would continue fighting but he would never again be a top contender. In 1978 he would suffer decision defeats to future middleweight champions Vito Antuofermo and Marvin Hagler.

Briscoe would continue fighting winning about half of his fights with elite fighters. Briscoe finally retired after losing a majority decision to Ralph Hollett in June of 1982.

Briscoe was considered by many boxing experts to be one of the greatest fighters to never win a world title. He was a powerful puncher with both hands, and he had an excellent left jab. He had a strong chin and was only knocked out once in his career. No less an expert then Carlos Monzon stated that Briscoe was probably the hardest puncher that he had ever faced; further stating that he had a lot of respect for him. When fighting in Europe, Briscoe was fondly called the "black robot" because of his mechanical ring style of always moving forward. Briscoe was most certainly loved in Philadelphia and maintained his sanitation department job up until his retirement from the ring.

Briscoe's final ring record was 66 wins, 24 losses and 5 draws. He won 53 fights by knockout giving him a knockout to win ratio of 80.3 per cent.

In 2003 Ring Magazine named Briscoe the 34th greatest knockout puncher of all time. In 2010 Briscoe was inducted into the World Boxing Hall of fame based in the Los Angeles, California area.

Briscoe passed away in 2010 in Philadelphia at 67 years of age after a short illness.

Eugene "Cyclone" Hart
Boxrec.com

Inductee # 9 EUGENE (CYCLONE) HART

Eugene (Cyclone) Hart was born on June 6, 1951, in Philadelphia, Pennsylvania. At the age of 2, Hart contracted polio, and to build his body up he took to amateur boxing.

In Philadelphia he belonged to The Champs gym and also the local Police Athletic league. As an amateur Hart compiled a record of 29 wins, and 3 losses. He won 9 fights by knockout.

While at an out-of-town amateur boxing contest one of the coaches told him that he fought like a cyclone, and he became known as Eugene (Cyclone) Hart.

Hart turned professional at the age of 18 by knocking out Sheldon Moore in one round in his professional debut at the Philadelphia Blue Horizon Venue on September 30, 1969.

While training in Philadelphia, Hart was able to spar with former welter weight and middleweight champion Emile Griffith, and with top contender Gypsy Joe Harris. He also sparred with Stanley (Kitten) Hayward, and Jesse Smith.

Fighting about once a month at the Blue Horizon Venue, he knocked out Sonny Gravely in 1 round in October of 1969, Al Thomas in 2 rounds in November of 1969, and veteran Art Kettles in 3 rounds to finish out 1969.

Hart's vicious left hook was responsible for all his quick knockouts. Hart threw his left hook like a sickle and, if it landed on target, the opponent was usually down for the full ten count.

Hart was drawing huge crowds at the Blue Horizon Venue where people came just to guess what round Hart would flash his left hook and take out his opponent.

Promoters at the Blue Horizon were having to pay preliminary fighters extra money just to come to Philadelphia and face Hart and his infamous left hook.

Hart continued in his winning ways much to the pleasure of his manager Sam Solomon. He began the year of 1969 by knocking out Sam Mosely in one round in January and Joe Williams in one round just two weeks later at the Blue Horizon.

In February of 1970 Hart knocked out Gene Masters at 2:51 of the first round to win his 3rd fight in a row by first round knockout.

Continuing his winning streak, Hart won his 8th fight in a row when he knocked out John Saunders in 3 rounds in March of 1970. Hart recorded another 3rd round knockout when he beat Vernon Mason in April of 1970.

In May of 1970 Hart knocked out Sonny Floyd with the first left hook he landed at the 58 second mark. Former opponent John Saunders unwisely asked for a rematch with Hart in Wilmington, Delaware in the latter part of May in 1970. Hart left Philadelphia and traveled to Delaware to knock Saunders out again in the 4th round.

Hart returned to the Blue Horizon Venue in Philadelphia to take out Humberto Trotman in 5 rounds in June of 1970.

Hart took 3 months off from fighting and did not return to the ring again until he knocked out Leroy Roberts in 4 rounds in September of 1970

Humberto Trotman made the same mistake as John Saunders when he asked for a rematch with the hard punching Hart in November of 1970. Hart needed only 2 rounds to knock out Trotman in the rematch at The Arena in Philadelphia. Hart then stopped opponent Dave Ditmar in 5 rounds at the Spectrum in Philadelphia in November of 1970.

Hart closed out 1970 by knocking out Jim Davis in 4 rounds at the Blue Horizon in Philadelphia. In January of 1971 he began the year by stopping Freddie Martinovich in 3 rounds at the same venue.

In March of 1971 Hart stopped Jim Meilleur in 4 rounds at the Arena to set up a huge cross town rivalry fight with another hot Philadelphia prospect, Stanley (Kitten) Hayward at The Arena in Philadelphia in May of 1971.

The fight was a huge event for the boxing public in Philadelphia, and Hart knocked Hayward out cold in the first round with the first left hook that he landed. At this point Hart was considered to be more than a hot prospect, but a legitimate top 10 contender in the middleweight division.

In June of 1971 former middleweight title challenger Don Fullmer became the first man to go the distance with Hart. Hart battered Fullmer around the ring to win a unanimous decision over the rugged middleweight contender.

In August of 1971 Hart climbed up the middleweight ratings as high as number 3 when he knocked out Fate Davis at the Spectrum in Philadelphia.

In September of 1971 top ranked middleweight contender Denny Moyer traveled to The Spectrum in Philadelphia to take on the unbeaten Hart. Moyer was a veteran of over 100 fights and, in 1962, he won what was called at the time the junior middleweight championship.

The fight started, and Hart dropped Moyer with a left hook in the 1st round. The wily veteran got up and survived the round. Moyer came back fighting but Hart was definitely the stronger puncher of the two. In the 6th round, the fighters became entangled in the ring ropes and fell out of the ring. Moyer suffered an ankle injury on the ring apron, but Hart was knocked unconscious when he landed on the concrete floor. The bout was declared a no-contest and Hart remained unbeaten.

Hart took 5 months off from the ring and returned in February of 1972 to knock out veteran Matt Donovan in 2 rounds at the Philadelphia Arena. It appeared that Hart was reluctant to fight near the ring ropes and he later stated that he had developed a fear of the ring ropes after the Moyer fight.

Hart had amassed a ring record of 22 wins, with 21 coming by knockout. He risked his number 3 ring ranking in the middleweight division when he took on another top ten contender in middleweight Nate Collins from San Francisco, California, in March of 1972 at the Philadelphia Arena.

Hart dropped Collins with a huge left hook in round 2 of the contest, and all the Philadelphia fight fans felt that Hart was going to add just one more opponent to his list of knockout victories.

Collins got up, cleared his head, and survived the 2nd round. Collins then began to counter punch Hart from a distance and stayed away from his left hook. Hart was tired by the 5th round from his earlier attempts to knock Collins out and his eyes began to swell from Collins jabs. By the 8th round, Hart had a hard time seeing out of his eyes and the fight was stopped. Hart had just suffered the first defeat of his career to the shock and surprise of the attending and adoring Philadelphia fans.

Hart's stamina was questioned after this fight by the Philadelphia press. Hart then turned to a new management team consisting of Cus D'Amato, and Jimmy Jacobs to enhance his ring career.

Hart took a whole year off from fighting and returned to the ring with his new management team in April of 1973 and took on the crafty veteran Jose Gonzalez.

It turned out that Gonzalez turned out to be too tough of an opponent to take on in his first comeback fight, and Hart was stopped again, this time in the 9th round, after taking an early lead in the fight.

Hart took off 4 months off after the Gonzales fight and returned to the ring in August of 1973 to knock out Thurman (Doc) Holliday) in 2 rounds at The Spectrum in Philadelphia.

In November of 1973 Hart knocked out Al Quinney in 2 rounds, to set up another big cross town rivalry fight with the slick boxing Willie (The Worm) Monroe in February of 1974. The fight was scheduled for The Spectrum in Philadelphia.

Monroe turned out to be too slick and crafty for Hart, as he danced and jabbed his way to a 10-round decision victory over the Philadelphia slugger.

Hart took off another 4 months from the ring to regroup and came back in July of 1974 to take on another local rival in Bobby (Boogaloo) Watts.

Watts caught Hart cold and knocked him out in the very first round. Just one month later in August, Hart made an ill-advised quick return to the ring to be knocked out in 4 rounds by future light heavyweight champion Eddie Mustapha Muhammed.

Hart took 5 months off from the ring and finally got back to his winning ways by knocking out Radames Cabrera in 8 rounds in January of 1975 at The Arena in Philadelphia.

In April, Hart stopped Mario Rosa in 4 rounds, and in June of 1975 he stopped Chucho Garcia. In August of 1975 Hart took on top middleweight contender Sugar Ray Seales in a nationally televised fight from Atlantic City, New Jersey. Seales had been an Olympics medalist and was the heavy favorite in the fight.

Hart punishing Sugar Ray Seales in a nationally televised fight
World Boxing, March 1976

Hart never looked better in the ring in front of a national audience. Hart showed power and stamina as he battered Seales around the ring and gave him a severe beating in winning a going away unanimous decision.

Hart returned to the Spectrum in Philadelphia in November of 1975 to take on Philadelphia middleweight legend Bennie Briscoe.

In what may have been the greatest fight of Hart's career, he traded bombs with Briscoe for the full 10 rounds before the fight was declared a draw by the judges. Hart was able to take punishment from Briscoe and deliver his own powerful left hooks for the full fight.

Hart was back in the middleweight rankings after his victory over Seales and his draw in Briscoe. In February of 1976 Hart would knock out Melvin Dennis in 3 rounds to set up a rematch with Briscoe in April of 1976.

Hart would prove to have a weak chin again, as Briscoe took him out in the first round of the rematch. It was beginning to look as though if Hart could not knock you out early in a fight, then he, in turn, would end up being a knockout victim. In his fights, usually somebody was going to get knocked out.

In August of 1976 Hart knocked out Matt Donovan to set up a big main event fight with the future middleweight champion Marvin Hagler at The Spectrum in September of 1976.

Hart tried and landed some of his left hook bombs on Hagler early in the fight, but Hagler had a steel chin and shrugged off Hart's powerful blows. Hart seemed to lose interest after the first 5 rounds, and Hagler came back to stop him in the 8th round of the exciting fight.

Hart took 6 months off from the ring and tried to regroup again by taking on another top contender and future middleweight champion named Vito Antuofermo in March of 1977 at the Arena in Philadelphia.

Hart came out firing left hooks in the first couple of rounds and rocked Antuofermo on several occasions. Antuofermo would later state that Hart's left hooks to the body were actually lifting his feet off of the ground. Antuofermo weathered the storm and waited until Hart had punched himself out. By the end of the 4th round, Hart was tired and came out for the 5th round on unsteady legs.

Antuofermo dropped Hart in the 5th round near the ropes and Hart was too tired to lift his body off of the canvas before the 10-count.

Antuofermo would state after the fight that he could feel the breeze of Hart's left hooks whistling by his head. After his retirement Antuofermo would state that Hart was the strongest puncher he ever fought. Antuofermo also added that Hart punched harder than Marvin Hagler.

Hart left the ring for 5 years and then made an ill-advised comeback when he was stopped by Tony Suero in Atlantic City, New Jersey in April of 1982.

Hart was the type of fighter that fight fans loved to watch. He won 30 fights, 28 by knockout, and he lost 9 fights, 8 by knockout. Hart won about 75 per cent of his fights with over 90 per cent of his wins coming by knockout. He lost about 25 per cent of his fights, and just about all of his losses were by knockout—if one attended a Hart fight, it was to see someone get knocked out as just about all of his fights ended by knockout. Thankfully, it was usually his opponents who were knocked out.

Hart is not a hall of fame fighter, and he was never even given a chance to fight for the title, however he was most definitely a hall of fame puncher.

Hart currently trains amateur fighters in Philadelphia and his son Jesse Hart is a top-notch super middleweight contender. Hart's his final ring record was 30 wins, 9 losses with 1 draw, and 1 no contest. He won 28 fights by knockout giving him a knockout to win ratio of 93.3 per cent.

The 2003 Ring magazine edition named Hart as the 61st greatest puncher in the history of the ring.

Thomas (Hitman) Hearns
KO Magazine. November 1984

Inductee # 10   THOMAS (HITMAN) HEARNS

Thomas Hearns was born on October 18th, 1958, in Grand Junction, Tennessee. At the age of 5, Hearns moved with his family to Detroit, Michigan.

Taking up the sport of boxing in Detroit, Hearns entered the KRONK gym, and, under the guidance of trainer Emanuel Steward, he compiled an amateur record of 155 wins and just 8 losses.

Hearns won a slew of national amateur Golden Gloves and Amateur Athletic Union (AAU) titles. In the amateurs, Hearns learned to be a master boxer but, as a professional, Steward turned his protégé into a devastating power puncher.

Tall for a welterweight at 6'1" in height, Steward turned Hearns into a power puncher by teaching him to put leverage on his punches in the ring. Hearns turned professional in November of 1977 by knocking out Jerome Hill at The Olympia Stadium in Detroit, Michigan.

Hearns, with his newfound punching power, knocked out all 17 of his opponents between 1977 and 1979. His knockout victims included some big-name fighters such as Eddie Marcelle, Bruce Finch, Pedro Rojas, Rudy Barro, and Clyde Gray.

In April of 1979 Alfonso Hayman became the first fighter to go the distance with Hearns. Hearns pitched a near shut out in winning a unanimous decision over Hayman at The Spectrum in Philadelphia.

In May of 1979 Hearns stopped another welterweight contender when he stopped Harold Weston in Las Vegas, Nevada. Weston suffered a detached retina and the fight had to be stopped at the end of the 6th round. After the fight, some questions were raised about Hearns stamina as he appeared to be fading in the fight just before Weston quit on his stool at the end of the 6th round.

In June of 1979 Hearns stopped contender Bruce Curry at the Olympia in Detroit Michigan. Then, in October, Hearns knocked down and stopped former super lightweight champion Saensak Muangsurin at The Olympia Stadium in Detroit, Michigan.

In November of 1979 Hearns dropped top middleweight contender Mike Colbert in the 2nd, 3rd ,5th, and 10th round on his way to a near shutout unanimous decision victory at the Superdome in New Orleans, Louisina.

After defeating former world champions Angel Espada and Eddie Gazo, Hearns issued a challenge to fight Pipino Cuevas, for his World Boxing Association welterweight title. Hearns entered the title fight with a record of being unbeaten in 28 consecutive fights.

The title fight with Cuevas was set for August 2nd, 1980, at the Joe Louis Arena in Detroit, Michigan. Cuevas had been the World Boxing Association welter weight champion at the age of 18 since 1976. Cuevas had made 12 successful defenses of his title and possessed a devastating left hook. The fight would be between Hearns powerful right hand versus Cuevas powerful left hook. As the fighters came to ring center for the pre-fight instructions from the referee Hearns at 6'1', towered over the shorter Cuevas at 5'9" in height.

In the opening round Hearns kept Cuevas at a distance with his long jab and drilled him with straight right hands to the head every time Cuevas would try to fight inside and land his left hook. Hearns staggered Cuevas with a right hand late in the round, but the bell rang before Hearns could finish him off.

Hearns came out for the 2nd round and immediately backed Cuevas into a corner. Cuevas would try to fight back, but he could not get inside to land his left hook. A straight right hand staggered Cuevas into doing a crazy dance and a follow up right hand to the head dropped him immediately, face first, to the canvas. Cuevas did get up before the 10-count, but after a few more Hearns right hands to his head, Cuevas' corner threw in the towel to stop the fight. The KRONK gym had another world champion for Detroit to be proud of.

In December of 1980 Hearns accepted the challenge of unbeaten Venezuelan contender Luis Primera. The title fight was set for the Joe Louis Arena in Detroit and Hearns knocked out Primera in the 6th round to the delight of the Detroit fight fans.

Ring Magazine gave Hearns the fighter of the year award for 1980. Not to rest on his laurels, Hearns was back in the ring in April of 1981 to defend his title. Slick boxing contender Randy Shields was his opponent. Shields lasted until round 12 when he was unable to continue because of cuts.

In June of 1981 Hearns was back in the ring again and knocked out fringe contender Pablo Baez in the 4th round in the Astrodome in Houston, Texas.

The stage was now set for a big welterweight title unification match between Hearns and the World Boxing Council Champion Sugar Ray Leonard in September of 1981. Leonard had been an Olympic Gold medalist and had only lost to Roberto Duran in

31 fights. Leonard had defeated Duran in a rematch. The fight would take place at Caesars Palace in Las Vegas, Nevada.

Hearns would turn boxer in the first part of the fight as he jabbed and counter punched his way to a big points lead in the early rounds. Leonard has his moments when he broke through with hard punches to seriously hurt Hearns in the 6th round. Hearns went back to boxing and had built up an even larger points lead by the end of the 12th round.

Hearns hammering Leonard with a right hand
Boxing 89. November 1989

Leonard's left eye was closing rapidly from Hearns pinpoint jabs and corner man Angelo Dundee implored Leonard to become aggressive and take the fight to Hearns again. Leonard followed Dundee's instructions and seriously hurt Hearns in the 13th round. Leonard knocked Hearns through the ropes for a 9 count at the bell ending the 13th round. Hearns appeared exhausted as he walked out of his corner for the 14th round on shaky legs. It was obvious that Hearns had not fully recovered from Leonard's 13th round beating. Leonard went right after Hearns to start the 14th round and nailed him with several unanswered combinations before the referee finally intervened and awarded the fight to Leonard.

Hearns blamed part of his loss on being drained trying to make the 147-pound limit. He solved this problem by moving up to the 154-pound super welterweight limit.

In December of 1981 Hearns defeated middleweight Ernie Singletary by decision and knocked out veteran middleweight Marcos Geraldo, in Las Vegas, in February of 1982.

In December of 1982 Hearns challenged World Boxing Council super-welterweight champion Wilfred Benitez for his title. In a classic matchup of two superb boxers, Hearns was able to win a majority decision and take the title from Benitez.

In February of 1984 Hearns defended his title and won a unanimous decision over Italian Luigi Minchillo in Detroit, Michigan.

In June of 1984 Hearns defended his title against the Latin legend Roberto Duran. Duran had never been knocked out in his ring career and was expected to test Hearns' chin.

Hearns landed a vicious right hand to Duran's head in the second round and Duran collapsed to the canvas, face first. Duran did not move a muscle throughout the whole 10-count. This fight was probably Hearns finest hour in the ring.

In September of 1984 Hearns defended against Fred Hutchings of Stockton, California. Hutchings had only lost once in 28 professional fights, and he had reversed his only loss prior to stepping into the ring with Hearns.

The fight was held in Saginaw, Michigan, and Hutchings seemed to be overwhelmed by the moment as he went down twice in the opening round. Hutchings fought timidly and he was hurt again when the fight was finally stopped in the 3rd round.

In April of 1985 Hearns moved up to the middleweight division in an attempt to take champion Marvin Hagler's crown. The title match was advertised as "The War". The fight lived up to everyone's expectations.

At the first bell, Hagler came right after Hearns and started slugging. Hearns had no alternative but to fight for his life in a life-or-death struggle. There was no time for the normal feeling out process. Both fighters threw over 80 punches in the first round with Hearns inflicting a cut between Hagler's eyes and winning a close first round.

Hagler stormed out of his corner for the 2nd round more determined than ever to end the fight by knockout. The 2nd round was a war similar to the first round and it looked like it just became an old-fashioned street fight between two sluggers. Hagler was obviously looking for the quick knockout and Hearns was beginning to look worn by the end of the second round due to the frantic pace that Hagler was setting.

The cut on Hagler's face was bleeding and the ringside doctor inspected the cut in his corner. Hagler was afraid that the fight would be stopped by the cut, and he charged after Hearns as the 3rd round started. Midway through the round, the referee stopped the action to check on Hagler's cut. The referee allowed the fight to continue, and Hagler charged after a tiring Hearns again, still afraid that the fight might be stopped due to his cut. Hagler landed a long right hand which caused Hearns to collapse to the canvas flat on his back. Hearns miraculously got off the canvas before the 10-count but was in no shape to continue the fight. The referee stopped the fight and awarded it to Hagler.

In the end, Hagler was the fighter with a better chin and thus the victor. Hearns took nearly 1 year off from the ring before returning in March of 1986 to fight James Shuler in Las Vegas, Nevada. Shuler was undefeated in 22 fights, and the fight was for the North American Boxing Federation middleweight title.

Hearns iced Shuler in the first round and Shuler was killed in a motorcycle accident one week after the fight. Hearns presented the North American Federation title belt to Shuler's family at his funeral as a sign of his respect and condolence.

In March of 1987 Hearns made a move up to the light heavyweight division and stopped Dennis Andres in the 10th round in Detroit, Michigan, to win the World Boxing Council light heavyweight title

In April of 1987 Sugar Ray Leonard defeated Marvin Hagler for the middleweight title, and it would be Hagler's last professional fight. Leonard did not seem to have much interest in defending the title and the various alphabet boxing organizations nominated their own fighters to fight for the title. The World Boxing Council chose Hearns and Argentina's Juan Domingo Roldan to fight for their version of the vacant middleweight title in October of 1987 in Las Vegas, Nevada.

Roldan had put up a good fight in challenging Marvin Hagler for the title in 1984, and had recently defeated James Kinchen to qualify for the title fight.

Hearns started off fast and dropped Roldan as he was coming towards him in the first round. Hearns continued to batter Roldan in the second round, but Roldan came back in the 3rd round to corner Hearns and hurt him with left hooks and roundhouse right hands.

Hearns appeared a bit unsteady as he came out for the 4th round, but he caught Roldan with a straight right hand counter punch that dropped Roldan face first to the canvas. Roldan took the 10-count on his stomach without moving a muscle. Roldan would later state that he heard the count but was too hurt and dazed to get up.

Hearns had now accumulated 4 world titles all the way from the welterweight title up to the light heavyweight title. His next middleweight title defense would be against New York's hard hitting middleweight Iran (The Blade) Barkley in January of 1988 in Las Vegas, Nevada.

Hearns, as his custom, started off fast and by the third round Barkley was bleeding badly and the fight appeared ready to be stopped. Barkley became desperate because of his cuts and unleashed a left hook and right hand that dropped Hearns near the ropes. Hearns was unable to continue, and the press began talking about Hearns "weak chin" in their post-fight press releases.

Hearns rebounded again to fight for the World Boxing Organizations super middleweight title in November of 1988, when he won a majority decision over the veteran James (The Heat) Kinchen in Las Vegas, Nevada. Even though he won the title, Hearns exhibited his customary excellent boxing skills, but he was severely hurt at one point. The only thing that prevented him from getting knocked out was when he held onto Kinchen for close to 30 seconds after being stung by a Kinchen punch and the referee was unable to break them apart. Hearns was penalized one point for holding, but he had bought time to clear his head and continue the fight. This was another occasion where Hearns ability to take a punch was criticized in both the press and by boxing analysts at ringside.

In June of 1989 Hearns was finally able to obtain a rematch with Sugar Ray Leonard. Hearns dropped Leonard twice during the fight and was staggered in the fight by Leonard but was able to remain upright. Hearns gained a measure of prestige from this fight, as he fought hard for the whole distance Many people felt that he actually deserved the decision in the close fight, instead of the judges' draw decision.

After a couple of tune up fights, Hearns then challenged unbeaten Champion Virgil Hill for his World Boxing Association light heavyweight title. Hearns obtained a new trainer in Alex Sherer, who had previously worked at the KRONK gym for Emanuel Steward in Detroit. The title fight was set for June of 1991 in Las Vegas, Nevada.

Under Sherer's guidance Hearns fought the perfect fight, by counter punching Hill effectively and keeping him off balance during the whole 12 round fight. Hearns won a unanimous decision and the World Boxing Association light heavyweight title.

In March of 1992 Hearns defended his light heavyweight title belt against old nemesis Iran (The Blade) Barkley in Las Vegas, Nevada. Hearns came out for the start of the first round boxing, but Barkley was able to muscle Hearns towards the ropes round after round where he dominated the infighting. Trainer Sherer pleaded with Hearns to stay off of the ropes, but Hearns either was unable to stay off the ropes or became comfortable counter punching from the ropes. In the end Hearns lost a split decision and the title to Barkley.

Hearns took more than a year off from boxing, and then returned in November of 1993 to knock out Andrew Maynard in Las Vegas, Nevada. In February of 1994 Hearns won a unanimous decision over Freddie Delgado in Charlotte, North Carolina for the

North American Boxing Federation Cruiserweight title. In March of 1995 Hearns would knock out Lennie LaPaglia for the World Boxing Union Cruiserweight title in Detroit, Michigan.

In April of 1999 Hearns would win a unanimous decision over Nate Miller for the vacant International Boxing Organization (IBO) Cruiserweight title in Manchester, England.

Hearns would lose his Cruiserweight title to Uriah Grant by a technical knockout when he twisted his ankle in the 3rd round and could not continue in April of 2000 in front of his adopted hometown fans in Detroit, Michigan. Hearns promised the fans that he would return to Detroit to fight again before he retired.

Hearns kept his promise in 2005 when he stopped John Long at the Cobo Arena in Detroit, Michigan. Hearns closed out his ring career by knocking out Shannon Landberg in February of 2006 at The Palace in Auburn Hills, Michigan.

Hearns' final ring record was 61 wins, 5 losses, and 1 draw. He won 48 fights by knockout, giving him a knockout to win percentage of 78.7 per cent.

Hearns was listed as the 18th greatest puncher of all time by the Ring magazines 2003 edition. Hearns was credited with winning 6 major weight division titles in his career. Hearns was inducted into the International Boxing Hall of Fame in 2012.

Hearns has been married to former model Renee Hearns, for over 40 years and has one son, Ronald Hearns, who followed in his father's footsteps to become a professional boxer. Hearns is also a reserve officer with the Detroit Police Department.

Marvin Hagler
Sports Illustrated (cover). October 18, 1982

Inductee # 11   MARVIN HAGLER

Marvelous Marvin Hagler was born as Marvin Nathaniel Hagler on May 23, 1954, in Newark, New Jersey. After experiencing the effects of a couple of major riots in Newark in 1967 and 1969, Hagler's mother moved the entire family to Brockton, Massachusetts.

Growing up as a teenager in Brockton, Hagler decided he wanted to learn amateur boxing, after getting beat up in a street fight after a party. Hagler eventually walked into a Brockton gym owned by Pat and Goody Petronelli.

Hagler lied about his age to enter a National Athletic Union (AAU) tournament, and eventually won the 165-pound division. Hagler compiled an amateur boxing record of 55 wins, and only one loss.

Hagler turned professional at the age of 19 in May of 1973 by knocking out Terry Ryan in Brockton, Massachusetts. In August of 1973 Hagler knocked out Muhammed Smith at the Arena in Brockton.

In October of 1973 Hagler was matched with unbeaten Dornell Wigfall. Wigfall just happened to be the person who had beaten up Hagler in the street fight before he started amateur boxing. Hagler exacted his revenge on Wigfall by winning a unanimous decision over the previously unbeaten fighter.

Hagler was unbeaten in 14 fights when he was matched with the unbeaten Olympic Gold Medalist Sugar Ray Seales in Boston in August of 1974. Seales was unbeaten in 21 professional fights and was a heavy favorite in the fight. Hagler pulled a big upset by winning a unanimous decision over the previously unbeaten Gold Medalist.

On November 16, 1974, Hagler knocked out George Green in Brockton. Then, on November 26th, he fought a rematch with Sugar Ray Seales in Seales' hometown of Seattle, Washington.

Hagler was held to a draw by Seales in what some boxing experts felt was a hometown decision by the local officials. In February of 1975 Hagler knocked out Dornell Wigfall in a rematch at the Brockton High School in Massachusetts.

Hagler would go on a 6-fight win streak. But his reputation made it hard to find any opponents who wanted to come to Boston, or Brockton, to fight him. In January of 1976 Hagler took on Bobby (Boogaloo) Watts in his hometown of Philadelphia, Pennsylvania. Hagler suffered his first defeat when Watts was given a 10 round majority decision victory.

Hagler returned to Boston in February of 1976 and knocked out Matt Donovan in his hometown. In March of 1976 Hagler returned to Philadelphia and took on slick boxing Willie (The Worm) Monroe at the Spectrum in Philadelphia. Monroe won a 10 round unanimous decision over Hagler. Hagler would later state that of the 3 losses that he had in his career, that this was the only fight that he thought he really lost.

In September of 1976 Hagler returned to Philadelphia to knock out hard punching Eugene (Cyclone) Hart in February of 1977 Hagler knocked out Willie (The Worm) Monroe in a rematch in Boston.

In August of 1977 Hagler traveled back to Philadelphia to knock out Monroe again in their rubber match. Hagler now found himself in the middleweight top ten rankings and boxing promoters from around the United States started to take notice of his accomplishments.

In November of 1977 Hagler took on unbeaten top ranked middleweight contender Mike Colbert in the Boston Garden, in Massachusetts. Hagler knocked out Colbert to take over the number one ranking in the middleweight division.

Hagler stayed busy by stopping England's Kevin Finnegan on cuts in Boston, Massachusetts in March of 1978. He went on to stop Doug Demmings in April of 1978 at the Olympic Auditorium in Los Angeles, California.

Kevin Finnegan foolishly asked Hagler for a rematch and they fought at the Boston Garden in May of 1978. Hagler stopped Finnegan one more time with cuts that would ultimately require 40 stitches to close.

In August of 1978 Hagler returned to Philadelphia to take on Philadelphia's top middleweight contender Bennie Briscoe. In the battle of the shaved heads, as it was billed, Hagler was too quick for the plodding Briscoe and won a clear cut 10 round decision.

In November of 1978 Hagler stopped tough Texas middleweight Willie Warren in 6 rounds, and then stopped Olympic Gold Medalist Sugar Ray Seales in the Boston Garden in February of 1979 in their rubber match.

Hagler was still the number 1 ranked middleweight contender, but it was Vito Antuofermo who received the first shot at the middleweight champion, Hugo Corro, in June of 1979 in Monte Carlo.

Vito Antuofermo took the middleweight title from Corro on a decision while Hagler knocked out Norberto Cabrera on the undercard. Hagler would finally get his title shot on November 30, 1979, in Las Vegas, Nevada against Antuofermo.

Hagler built up an early lead in his title fight challenge by bouncing combinations off Antuofermo's head and Antuofermo was cut immediately. Hagler seemed to coast in the middle rounds and allowed Antuofermo to get back into the fight. In the late rounds, Hagler allowed Antuofermo to back him up. At the end of 15 rounds, it appeared that Hagler had won enough early and middle rounds to get the decision, however the official verdict was a draw and Anutofermo kept his title.

Hagler was frustrated by the decision, and he returned to the ring to knock out contender Loucif Hamani in February of 1980 in Portland, Oregon.

In April of 1980 Hagler returned to Portland, Oregon, to knock out Bobby (Boogaloo) Watts. Hagler had now reversed both of his previous losses and he was ready to challenge for the middleweight title again.

Antuofermo had lost his middleweight title to England's Alan Minter in March of 1980 in Las Vegas. Hagler prepped for his title fight with Minter by winning a unanimous decision over tough guy Mexican Marcos Geraldo in May of 1980 in Las Vegas, Nevada.

In September of 1980 Hagler traveled to London, England, to challenge Alan Minter for the middleweight title. Racial tensions started before the fight as Minter was accused of making derogatory racial remarks towards Hagler.

Both fighters came out exchanging blows in a fairly even first round. Hagler started counter punching effectively in the second round and opened cuts on Minter's face. Hagler was battering a blood smeared Minter in the 3rd round when the referee called a halt to the contest and awarded the match and the title to Hagler.

As soon as the fight was stopped, pro-Minter British boxing fans began throwing bottles and cups into the ring. Hagler and his team had to be escorted out of the ring for their own protection. Hagler vowed never to return to England to fight, and he never did.

Hagler became a very busy champion as he knocked out undefeated Venezuelan Fulgencio Obel Mejias in January of 1981 in the Boston Garden.

In June of 1981 Hagler gave former champion Vito Antuofermo a rematch in the Boston Garden. Hagler dropped Antuofermo and stopped him in 5 rounds due to severe facial cuts.

In October of 1981 Hagler defended his title against top Syrian contender Mustafa Hamsho in Rosemont, Illinois. In a rough and tumble fight, Hamsho lasted until the 11th round before losing by a technical knockout due to cuts.

In March of 1982 Hagler took on William "Caveman" Lee in Atlantic City, New Jersey. Lee was a wild swinging knockout puncher who came right at Hagler at the start of the fight. Hagler did not have to go looking for Lee as he stood right in front of him. Hagler took out Lee before the 1st round was even half over.

In October of 1982 Hagler gave Fulgencio Obel Mejias a rematch in San Remo, Italy. Hagler knocked out Obel Mejias again in much quicker and easier fashion in their rematch.

In February of 1983 Hagler defended against England's roughhouse contender Tony Sibson in Worcester, Massachusetts. Sibson had also knocked out countryman Alan Minter and he was expected to test Hagler in the ring. Sibson was not much of a test as Hagler knocked him silly inside of 5 rounds.

In May of 1983 Hagler stopped fringe contender Wilford Scypion in Providence, Rhode Island. In November of 1983 Hagler finally had a big-name opponent to defend against in Panamanian legend Roberto Duran. Duran had been a lightweight champion, a welterweight champion, and he was currently a super welterweight champion at fight time. The fight with Duran would take place at Las Vegas, Nevada.

Duran put up a tough fight and they fought on even terms throughout the first 10 rounds. At the end of the 13th round, Duran was ahead on the scorecards. Hagler had to go all out and win the last 2 rounds to win a very close unanimous decision. The fight was somewhat of a disappointment for Hagler as he was expected to handle the smaller Duran much easier in the ring

In March of 1984 Hagler had another tough middleweight title defense when he took on Argentine slugger Juan Domingo Roldan in Las Vegas, Nevada

Roldan started strong and was given credit for a knockdown in the first round in what appeared to be more of a push or shove that sent Hagler to the canvas. Hagler started to come on strong in the middle rounds as Roldan had one of his eyes start to close. Hagler knocked Roldan down in the 10th round with a combination. Roldan beat the 10-count, but he then advised the referee that he could not see out of his damaged eye and did not wish to continue. Hagler won by a 10th round technical knockout.

In October of 1984 Hagler gave Mustafa Hamsho a rematch in Madison Square Garden, New York. Hagler became angry when

Hamsho continually head butted him and he took out Hamsho with a furious combination in the 3rd round.

Super welterweight champion Thomas "Hitman" Hearns had been calling for a middleweight title fight, and Hagler finally agreed to terms to defend his title against the Super welterweight champion. The fight was set for April 15, 1985, in Las Vegas, Nevada. The predictions for the potentially epic fight led to its advertisement as "The War".

Both fighters were knockout punchers, and the fight was not expected to last the distance. The fight was indeed "a war" as Hagler came out for the first round at full speed looking for the immediate knockout. Hearns fought back hard to defend himself and stunned Hagler in the first round and cut him on the forehead with a right-hand punch.

Hagler came out even stronger in the second round as he chased the weakened Hearns around the ring. Hearns fought back, but he went back to his corner at the end of the round on shaky legs.

Hagler resumed the attack in the 3rd round, but the referee stopped the fight to have the doctor check the cut on Hagler's face. The doctor allowed the fight to continue with Hagler still bleeding from the cut. Afraid that the fight might be stopped on cuts. Hagler went all out for the knockout and clubbed Hearns on the side of the head with a right hand that sent him straight to the canvas on his back. Hearns laid still and then suddenly jumped up to beat the full count It was obvious that Hearns was in no shape to continue the fight and Hagler was awarded a 3rd round technical knockout victory in a classic fight.

Hagler scores his career-defining win over Tommy Hearns
The Ring Magazine 2003 Yearbook; The 100 Greatest Punchers

Hagler took all most a year off from the ring and did not return to the ring until March of 1986 in Las Vegas, Nevada. Hagler's challenger was John "The Beast" Mugabi, a hard punching Ugandan challenger.

The fight itself was brutal as both fighters hammered each other for 10 vicious rounds. In the 11th round, Mugabi could take no more punishment and finally succumbed to Hagler's consistent attack.

Hagler was aging and slowing down in the ring, but he could not pass up the opportunity to defend his title against boxing's glamour boy Sugar Ray Leonard.

Leonard had not fought for close to 3 years, even though he stayed in training for much of that time. Leonard wanted the fight to be contested at 12 rounds, and Hagler agreed. The fight was set for April of 1987 in Las Vegas, Nevada. This would be Leonard's first fight in the middleweight division.

Leonard started off boxing well as Hagler did next to nothing in the first two rounds. Hagler became more aggressive in the 3rd round and the two warriors fought on even terms up through round 10. Hagler chased after Leonard in the last two rounds and Leonard fought back with late round eye-catching fast flurries. The fight would go to the scorecards where Leonard was given a 12-round split decision victory. Leonard had sprung the upset, and many boxing experts were divided on who actually won the fight. Hagler was irate and felt that he had been robbed of his title. Hagler felt that he was the aggressor for the whole 12 rounds and landed the harder blows. Hagler asked for a rematch, but Leonard would not give him one. Fed up with a titleholder getting to choose his opponents, Hagler retired from the ring for good.

In retirement Hagler moved to Italy and starred in adventure movies. Hagler would get divorced, and eventually marry an Italian woman, and live in Piotello, Italy.

In 1993 Hagler was inducted into the International Boxing Hall of Fame. In 2003 the Ring Magazine listed Hagler as the 35th greatest puncher of all time.

Hagler is generally recognized as one of the 5 greatest middleweight champions of all time. He was a vicious combination puncher who could take an opponent out with either hand. He was also known to have a granite chin in the ring.

Hagler passed away unexpectedly at the age of 66 in 2021. His final ring record was 62 wins, 3 losses, and 2 draws. He won 52 fights by knockout giving him a knockout to win percentage of 88.9 per cent.

Julian Jackson
The Ring Magazine 2003 Yearbook; The 100 Greatest Punchers

Inductee # 12   JULIAN JACKSON

Julian Jackson was born on September 12th, 1960, in Saint Thomas of the U.S. Virgin Islands. Jackson first became interested in boxing around age 14 when he followed a friend into amateur boxing.

Jackson professed to having 17 amateur fights and winning 15 of them. Jackson represented the Virgin Islands in the 1979 Pan American Games but would lose his first fight.

Jackson would make his professional debut on February 2, 1981, by winning a 4-round decision over Inocencio Carmona in San Juan, Puerto Rico.

Jackson would win his next 2 fights by knockout and then come home to the Virgin Islands and knock out Reyes Escalera in 3 rounds in St. Thomas.

In August of 1981 Jackson knocked out Edwin Rodriguez in 1 round in San Juan, Puerto Rico, and then traveled to Miami Beach, Florida, to stop Dario De Asa in 3 rounds in September of 1981.

In March of 1982 Jackson was forced to go the distance in winning a 6-round decision from William Page in Atlantic City, New Jersey.

Jackson closed out 1982 by knocking out Miguel Sepulveda in August, and Mack Heinbaugh in November in St. Joseph, Missouri. Jackson moved up to the 10 round main event fights in February of 1983 where he knocked out Dominic Fox in 2 rounds in Puerto Rico.

Jackson would knock out all 5 of his opponents in 1983 and his record would stand at 15 wins, no losses, and 13 wins by knockout. Promoters Don King and Bob Arum began taking notice of Jackson's one punch knockout power.

Jackson was knocking out opponents with his left or right hand. Jackson could also be a one punch knockout artist.

Jackson began fighting ranked light middleweight contenders in 1984 by knocking out Colton Brown in January, Eddie Gazo in March, and J.J. Cottrell in May.

In June of 1984 Jackson stopped Ron Lee Warrior in 3 rounds to win the World Boxing Council Continental Americas light middleweight title in San Juan, Puerto Rico.

Jackson retained his title by stopping Curtis Ramsey in the 12th round in Winchester, Nevada, to bring his undefeated record to 20 wins and no losses.

Jackson defended his title twice in November of 1984. He stopped Santos Solis in 2 rounds on November 3rd in Puerto Rico, and Sacramento, California's Tim Harris in 8 rounds on November 21st in Winchester, Nevada.

Jackson would take 6 months off from the ring before returning to knock out Rafael Corona in 3 rounds in July of 1985 in Santa Clara, California.

Jackson would fight twice more in 1985 knocking out Jose Padilla in 3 rounds in Winchester, Nevada. In November he knocked out Raul Hernandez in 1 round in Miami, Florida. Jackson was now ranked in the top ten of light middleweight contenders and was looking for a title fight against champion Mike (The Body Snatcher) McCallum.

Jackson knocked out Lopez McGee in 4 rounds in February of 1986 in the Virgin Islands. Jackson then knocked out Mark Allman in March, Francisco Del Toro in April, and Derrick Drane in May before challenging World Boxing Association light middleweight champion Mike McCallum in August of 1986 in Miami Beach, Florida.

At the beginning of round one, Jackson came out looking for his customary knockout victory and he rocked McCallum a couple of times before the round ended. In round two, the veteran McCallum began timing Jackson's rushes and counter punched him into a 2nd round technical knockout victory. Jackson's style of bum rushing his opponents with no regard for defense cost him the title against the wily McCallum. Jackson's record now stood at 29 wins, and 1 defeat.

McCallum then moved up to the middleweight division and Jackson had another opportunity to challenge for the vacant light middleweight title in November of 1987 against Korean In-Chul Baek in Las Vegas, Nevada.

Jackson knocked Baek out in the 3rd round to win the World Boxing Association light middleweight title. Jackson's record now stood at 32 wins with just 1 loss.

In July of 1988 Jackson scored a one-punch knockout victory over Buster Drayton in 3 rounds in Atlantic City, New Jersey. At this point, promoter Don King made sure Jackson's fights were being televised worldwide for everyone to see his incredible punching power.

In February of 1989 Jackson scored another one punch knockout over Brazilian Francisco de Jesus in 8 rounds in Las Vegas, Nevada. In July of 1989 Jackson had his first high profile fight against another topflight light middleweight contender in Terry Norris.

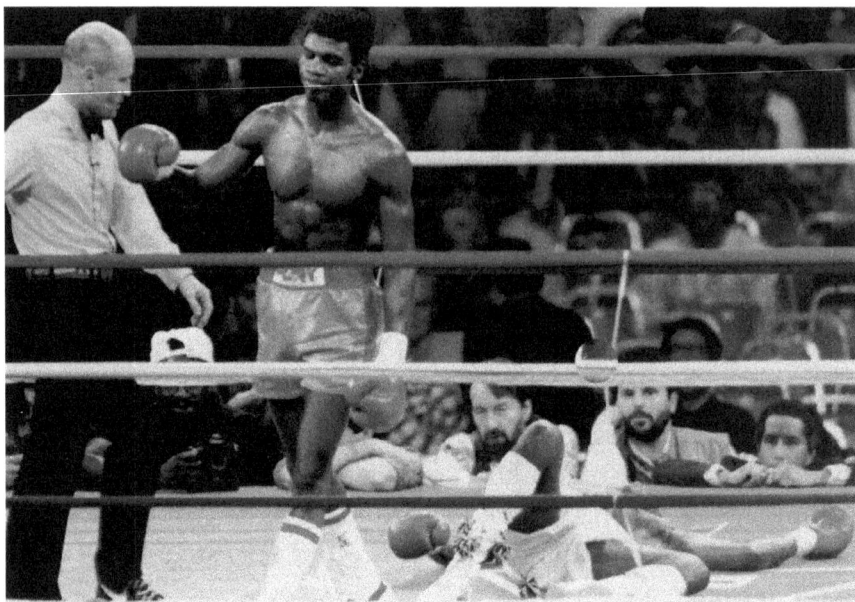

"The Hawk" starches Fransisco de Jesus in 8
The Ring Magazine 2003 Yearbook; The 100 Greatest Punchers

In a classic showdown between two knockout specialists, Jackson struck first and froze Norris with a right to the jaw in the second round which left him knocked out standing up. A second right hand knocked him through the ropes and left him unconscious for a spectacular knockout victory.

Jackson then challenged Sugar Ray Leonard for a big money fight, but Leonard wisely ignored Jackson's challenge. Wanting a challenge, Jackson decided to move up to the middleweight division and challenge England's number one contender Herol Graham for the vacant middleweight title.

Jackson had recent eye surgery to repair a detached retina and English officials would not allow him to compete in England. The fight for the vacant title was, therefore, moved to Spain where there was no protest from the officials.

Graham easily outboxed Jackson for the first 3 rounds and had him cut and bleeding. In the 4th round Graham backed Jackson into the ropes to try and deliver the knockout punch when Jackson lashed out with an overhand right hand counter punch that knocked Graham out cold for 5 minutes in the ring. Jackson, with one powerful punch, became the new World Boxing Council middleweight champion.

Jackson took 10 months off from the ring to allow his facial injuries to heal before he defended his middleweight title against Dennis Milton in September of 1991 in Nevada.

The title fight did not last long as Jackson blasted Milton out with the first powerful right hand that Jackson threw when the first round was just 2 minutes old.

In February of 1992 Jackson scored another one-round knockout when he took Ismael Negron out in just 50 seconds of their title fight in Paradise, Nevada.

In August of 1992 Jackson had to go 12 tough rounds to win a decision over rugged contender Thomas Tate. Jackson not only showed punching power in this fight, but he also showed that he had stamina.

In May of 1993 Jackson defended against another power puncher in Detroit's Gerald McClellan. Jackson rushed out at the bell, but McClellan stood his ground and exchanged power punches with the champion for 4 rounds. McClellan was a tremendous right-hand puncher and eventually wore Jackson down for a 5th round knockout victory.

Jackson returned to the ring and scored a couple of knockout victories before he won a unanimous decision over Eduardo Ayala in May of 1994 in Paradise, Nevada.

Jackson then challenged McClellan to a rematch for the middleweight title in May of 1994 in Paradise, Nevada. McClellan was all over Jackson from the opening bell and did not give him a chance to get set to throw a powerful punch. McClellan dropped Jackson and then stopped him in the middle of the first round. McClellan then vacated the title and moved up to the super middleweight division.

Jackson was next matched with the Italian European middleweight champion Agostino Cardamone for the vacant middleweight title in March of 1995 in Worcester, Massachusetts. Cardamone was undefeated in 23 fights and was a slight favorite in the fight.

Cardamone stunned and cut Jackson in the first round, but Jackson was able to survive to the final bell. Cardamone came out aggressively in the second round looking for the knockout when Jackson hit him with a looping right hand to the jaw that dropped him flat on his back, with his feet flying in the air. Somehow Cardamone got up before the 10-count. The referee noticed that he was unsteady on his feet and stopped the fight. Jackson was now a two-time middleweight champion.

The last thing a fighter loses in the ring is his punch, and when Jackson defended his title against Quincy Taylor in August of 1995, that is all he had left when he lost on a 6th round technical knockout

Jackson would win a couple of decisions over Leonardo Aguilar, and Augustine Renteria to close out 1996. In August of 1997 Jackson would knock out Terry Ford, and Eduardo Guttierez to set up a fight in January of 1998 against Verno Phillips for the lightly regarded World Boxing Union light middleweight title.

Phillips stopped Jackson in the 9th round of their title fight held in Robinsonville, Mississippi.

In May of 1998 Jackson was stopped by Anthony Jones in Auburn Hills, Michigan, in what became the final fight of his ring career.

Jackson would go down as one of the hardest punching middleweight champions in history and many boxing experts consider Julian (The Hawk) Jackson as the hardest punching middleweight champion of all time as devastation was housed in both of his hands.

When asked how he developed such tremendous punching power, Jackson would just state that it came natural to him as punchers were just born that way.

Jackson's final ring record was 55 wins, and 6 losses. He won 49 fights by knockout for an 89.1 knockout to win percentage.

In 2003 Ring Magazine considered Jackson the 25th hardest punching fighter in ring history.

Upon retirement Jackson joined the ministry in the Virgin Islands and trains two of his sons who have turned professional in the ring.

Jackson was inducted into the International Boxing Hall of Fame in 2019.

Gerald McClellan
The Ring Magazine 2003 Yearbook; The 100 Greatest Punchers

Inductee # 13   GERALD McCLELLAN

Gerald McClellan was born on October 23, 1967, in Freeport, Illinois. As an amateur he was a four-time Wisconsin Golden Gloves champion between 1984 and 1987. In 1987 he won the 156-pound division of the United States National Championships held in Buffalo, New York.

McClellan turned professional under the guidance of Emanuel Steward of the famed KRONK gym in Detroit, Michigan. McClellan turned professional on August 12, 1988, by knocking out Roy Hundley in 1 round in Milwaukee, Wisconsin.

McClellan showed incredible right-hand power even as a young professional by knocking out his first 10 opponents in either the first or second round.

McClellan suffered his first loss when Dennis Milton bested him and won a 6-round decision in Atlantic City, New Jersey, on January 24, 1989.

McClellan returned to the ring in September of 1989 and lost a unanimous 8 round decision to Ralph Ward in Atlantic City, New Jersey.

Under Emanuel Steward's guidance McClellan began showing his power punching skills by knocking out his next 3 opponents in the first round.

In December of 1989 he knocked out Rick Caldwell in one round in Saginaw, Michigan. He began the new year similarly when, in January of 1990, he knocked out James Williamson in the first round in Auburn Hills, Michigan. In March of 1990 he starched Ron Martin in one round in Bristol, Tennessee.

In April of 1990 McClellan stopped Brinatty Maquilon in three rounds in Atlantic City, New Jersey, and James Fernandez in two rounds in June of 1990 in Metairie, Louisiana.

In August of 1990 McClellan had to travel the 8-round distance to win a decision over shifty Sanderline Williams. Then, in September of 1990, he won an 8-round decision over Charles Hollis.

The Hollis fight would be the last time in McClellan's career that any of his fights would ever go the distance.

In November of 1990 McClellan pushed his record to 30 wins and 2 losses by knocking out Jose da Silva in three rounds in Phoenix, Arizona.

In December of 1990 McClellan knocked out Danny Mitchell in the first round and he also took out Ken Hulsey in one round in March of 1991 in Duluth, Minnesota.

Boxing authorities began to take notice of McClellan's punching power and he began to be ranked in the top ten in the middleweight division.

In July of 1991 McClellan took out Ivory Teague in 3 rounds in Norfolk, Virginia. Two weeks later he knocked out Sammy Brooks in one round in Auburn Hills, Michigan.

McClellan shocks Ivory Teague with a hard left jab
The Ring Magazine 2003 Yearbook; The 100 Greatest Punchers

In November of 1991 McClellan was matched against Ugandan top contender John (The Beast) Mugabi for the World Boxing Organization middleweight title at Royal Albert Hall in London, England.

Mugabi was a former World Boxing Council super-welterweight champion and had previously given Marvin Hagler a very tough fight for his World Middleweight crown.

McClellan and Mugabi were both known for their incredible punching power and boxing fans were expecting a slugfest.

The fans at Royal Albert Hall were not disappointed as McClellan came running out of his corner at the beginning of the fight and dropped Mugabi 3 times in the opening round for a technical knockout victory. McClellan had become the World Boxing Organization middleweight champion in only his 25th professional fight.

Due to McClellan's incredible punching power, he found it difficult to even find opponents who wanted to challenge for his middleweight title.

McClellan spent all of 1992 fighting in non-title fights. In February he knocked out Lester Yarbrough in one round and in May he stopped Carl Sullivan also in the 1st round.

In November McClellan knocked out Steve Harvey for his 3rd straight one-round knockout victory.

In February of 1993 McClellan traveled to Mexico City to knock out Tyrone Moore in 2 rounds.

In May of 1993 McClellan challenged World Boxing Council middleweight champion Julian Jackson for his title in Las Vegas, Nevada.

The McClellan versus Jackson fight promised to be an all-out punchers duel as both fighters had incredible one punch knockout power. The fight turned out to be a fight that fans dream of watching.

McClellan eventually proved to be the superior boxer as he stopped Jackson in the 5th round after both fighters had taken severe punishment from vicious head shots.

After winning the World Boxing Council middleweight title from Jackson, McClellan had no trouble finding challengers for the title.

McClellan became even more furious in the ring after becoming champion. In August of 1993, McClellan knocked out Jay Bell in one round in Bayamon, Puerto Rico.

In March of 1994 McClellan stopped veteran Gilbert Baptist in the first round in the 2nd defense of his title in Las Vegas, Nevada.

Two months later, in May of 1994, McClellan agreed to give Julian Jackson a rematch for the title in Las Vegas, Nevada.

The rematch turned out to be strictly no contest as McClellan stormed out of his corner at the start of the match and went all out for the knockout in the first minute of the fight. McClellan gave Jackson no chance to get set to punch as McClellan rained punches nonstop on Jackson until he collapsed to the floor. Jackson slumped to his knees with his head buried, face down, on the canvas. Jackson did not move until he was counted out by the referee.

After the Jackson rematch, McClellan decided to move up to the super middleweight division and challenge champion Nigel Benn of England.

McClellan had no problem putting on the extra weight for the fight as he frequently entered the ring weighing as much as 175 pounds. Julian Jackson later stated that McClellan looked like a light heavyweight in the ring after their Las Vegas rematch.

The title fight with Benn was set for February 25, 1995, in London, England. Due to McClellan's punching power, he was installed by the book makers as the favorite in the fight.

Benn was the hometown hero; however, he was a decided underdog in the fight. McClellan predicted his usual quick knockout in the pre-fight buildup to the contest.

As usual, McClellan came storming out of his corner looking for the first-round knockout and he almost got it. A flurry of hard right hands sent Benn tumbling through the ropes onto the ring apron in the first minute of the fight.

Ringsiders, seated by the ring apron, helped push Benn back into the ring just before the referee counted to 10. The referee gave Benn more time to recover by slowly waving the fighters together to begin fighting again. Benn managed to bob and weave away from McClellan's right-hand bombs to safely make it to the end of the first round.

Benn fought back on almost even terms with McClellan, who appeared to be fighting with his mouth open and mouthpiece exposed.

Finally, in the 8th round, McClellan appeared to have finally broken through Benn's defense and landed a straight long right hand to drop Benn to the canvas near the ropes.

Benn arose, groggy, from the canvas; but he proved to be a real warrior as he again used his ring guile to survive until the end of the round.

Benn came back fighting in the 9th round by launching a desperate attack which included landing a left hook and an accidental head butt which caused McClellan to start blinking his eyes. McClellan went down to one knee due to the pain, but the referee ordered him back up to fight.

In the 10th round, Benn landed a left hand and McClellan sank to one knee. McClellan got up to beat the 10-count, but approximately 30 seconds later Benn landed another left hand and McClellan went down to one knee again, took the full 10-count before he got up, and walked to his corner. Benn was declared the winner by a knockout by the referee to the delight of the British crowd.

To the casual fight observer, it appeared that McClellan just gave up in the fight, but after returning to his corner he slumped to the canvas and lost consciousness.

Ringside physicians provided lifesaving emergency treatment to McClellan until he could be transported to a hospital where a blood clot was surgically removed from the right side of his brain. McClellan's ring career was over, tragically and irreparably, in an instant.

McClellan suffered permanent damage from the fight including blindness, his ability to walk, and some deafness. As of this writing, McClellan has a sister who cares for him in Freeport, Illinois and various ring organizations have held fundraisers to help with his medical costs.

After his ring career was over there were reports that McClellan at one time had engaged in pit bull dog fights and at one time actually taped the mouth of a Labrador dog so it could be mauled and killed by his own pit bull fighting dog for training purposes.

Along with his pit bull fighting escapades, McClellan will always be known alongside Nigel Benn as being one of the two participants involved in one of the most savage bouts in ring history

McClellan, along with Nigel Benn and Julian Jackson were the most potent middleweight punchers of the 1990's. McClellan also had one of the highest rate of first round knockout wins of all middleweight champions.

In 2003 Ring magazine named McClellan as the 27th greatest puncher in ring history.

In 2007 McClellan was inducted into California's now defunct World Boxing Hall of Fame.

McClellan's final ring record was 31 wins, and 3 losses. He won 29 fights by knockout for a knockout to win ratio of 93.5 per cent.

Nigel Benn
The Ring Magazine. February 1993

Inductee 14 NIGEL BENN

Nigel Gregory Benn was born on January 22, 1964, in East London, England. Benn joined the British Army at the age of 18 and was stationed in West Germany for 3 years and in Northern Ireland for 18 months.

After leaving the Army he joined the West Ham Amateur Boxing Club and, in 1986, he was the amateur Boxing Association middleweight champion.

Benn turned professional in January of 1987 by knocking out Graeme Ahmed in Croydon, England. He then began a streak of 22 consecutive knockouts, including a 2-round technical knockout of Abdul Umaru Sanda in April of 1988 for the British Commonwealth middleweight title.

Benn defended his Commonwealth title successfully on three occasions. In October of 1988 he knocked out Anthony Logan in 12 rounds and in December he knocked out David Noel in the first round. Benn made his third successful title defense against Michael Chilambe by knocking him out in one round in Royal Albert Hall in London, England.

In May of 1989 Benn took his undefeated record of 22 wins, with all wins coming by knockout, into the ring with him to defend his Commonwealth title against British world ranked middleweight

Michael Watson. Watson had suffered only one defeat in 23 contests and was an accomplished boxer. The fight was held in London, England and the fight drew heavy media coverage.

Benn came out aggressively, but Watson was able to avoid most of Benn's power punches and countered him effectively. As the fight wore on Benn appeared to be frustrated as he lost stamina.

Benn appeared to have punched himself out and Watson actually dropped Benn to the floor with a hard straight jab in the 6th round. Benn was counted out as he arose from the canvas. The fight was over, and Watson had broken Benn's unbeaten streak and given him a boxing lesson.

In October of 1989 Benn fought for the first time in the United States and went the 10-round distance for the first time by winning a decision over Jorge Amparo in Atlantic City, New Jersey.

In January of 1990 Benn struggled to win a 10-round split decision over veteran Sanderline Williams in Atlantic City, New Jersey.

In April of 1989 Benn was nominated to challenge champion Doug DeWitt for the newly created World Boxing Organization's middleweight title in a nationally televised fight in Atlantic City, New Jersey. Benn did not let his supporters down as he dropped DeWitt and broke his ear drum on the way to a title winning 8th round technical knockout win.

Benn defeats DeWitt for the WBO middleweight title
KO Magazine. September 1990

In August of 1990 Benn traveled to Las Vegas, Nevada to defend his belt against top ranked heavy hitting contender Iran (The Blade) Barkley.

Benn jumped all over Barkley as the bell rang to begin the first round. Benn dropped Barkley 3 times in the first round for an automatic technical knockout victory. Benn was criticized in the American and British Press for hitting Barkley a couple of times while he was still on the canvas. Some boxing authorities felt that Benn should have been disqualified by the referee.

At the post-fight press conference Benn stated that he did not want to leave the American public with the impression that British fighters were not tough enough to compete with American fighters in the ring. His post-fight press conference comments drew even more criticism from the press.

In November of 1990 Benn again showed his lack of stamina when, British countryman, Chris Eubank outlasted him in a slug fest to take his middleweight title in a 9th round technical knockout in Birmingham, England.

Benn had been struggling to make the 160-pound limit and he decided to move up to the 168-pound super middleweight division to compete for a world title.

In April of 1991 Benn knocked out Marvin Hagler's half-brother Robbie Sims in 7 rounds in London, England.

Benn won his next 4 fights before taking on Thulane Malinga in a super middleweight title eliminator match in May of 1992 in Birmingham, England. Benn eked out a split decision victory over the crafty Malinga to earn a chance to fight champion Mauro Galvano for the World Boxing Council Super Middleweight title.

Benn challenged Galvano in October of 1992 in Marino, Italy, for the champion's title. Benn won the World Boxing Council super-middleweight fight when Galvano had to retire in the 4th round due to a severe eye cut. Benn was now a two-time champion.

In December of 1992 Benn defended his title against Nicky Piper in London, England. Benn battered Piper and stopped him in the 11th round for a technical knockout victory.

In March of 1993 Benn gave Mauro Galvano a rematch for the title in Glasgow, Scotland. Benn battered Galvano for 12 rounds to win a lop-sided decision over the defensive minded Italian.

In June of 1993 Benn returned to Kensington, England, and easily knocked out Lou Gent in 4 rounds, to tune up for a rematch with World Boxing Organization's super middleweight champion Chris Eubank.

The rematch with Eubank was finally set for Manchester, England in October of 1993. Benn entered the ring with a shaved head and a serious look on his face to defend his World Boxing

Council super-middleweight title. Benn fought with grit and determination to hold Eubank to a hotly contested 12 round draw. Both champions kept their respective belts and some ringside observers actually felt that Benn had won the fight.

Benn gained immense prestige from the British press with the gallant fight he put up with Eubank in defense of his title. Benn flashed his power and proved to have gained enough stamina to fight full speed for 12 rounds.

Benn next defended his title against challenger Harry Wharton in February of 1994 in London, England.

Benn looked sharp as he took a 12 round unanimous decision over Wharton and even better when he defended his title against Juan Carlos Giminez in September of 1994 in Birmingham, England. Benn took an impressive unanimous decision from Giminez to set the stage for a big money title defense against American challenger Gerald McClellan.

The title match with McClellan was set for February of 1995 in London, England. McClellan was an impressive knockout artist, as has been seen in the previous chapter, who had many first-round knockouts to his credit. McClellan was installed as a pre-fight favorite in the fight by the London bookmakers due to two recent impressive knockouts of Julian Jackson. McClellan also made statements to the press that he was predicting a win by an early-round knockout.

McClellan came out strong in the first round looking for the early knockout and Benn appeared surprised by the attack. McClellan trapped Benn along the ropes and threw a series of right hands which knocked him through the ropes and onto the ring apron.

Benn became entangled in the ropes, and it appeared like he would not be able to beat the 10-count.

Benn was assisted by ringside observers to get up and climb back into the ring just before the referee's ten count. Benn, as if by a miracle survived the first round by bobbing and weaving underneath McClellan's heavy artillery.

Benn came out strong in the second round and the two warriors took turns rocking each other with power punches, and they battled on even terms until the 8th round.

McClellan nailed Benn with a long straight right hand that dropped Benn near the ring ropes. Benn got up and held McClellan off until the round ended.

McClellan appeared to be tiring and was fighting with his mouth open and his mouthpiece hanging out of his mouth. Benn landed a left hook and his momentum carried him into McClellan — where Benn's head seemed to make contact with McClellan's face. McClellan appeared to start blinking his eyes after the accidental head butt.

McClellan came out for the 10th round in a weakened state and dropped to one knee after receiving a left hook from Benn. McClellan got up but, after another left hand from Benn, collapsed to one knee again. McClellan took the whole 10-count on one knee, and then got up and walked back to his corner. The London crowd erupted with joy. Benn was the winner by knockout in 10 rounds of all-out fighting.

After arriving at his corner McClellan collapsed into unconsciousness and had to be rushed to a local hospital where emergency surgery was performed to remove a blood clot from his brain. McClellan received permanent injuries from the bout, and he would never fight again.

Benn's victory showed him to be a brilliant champion who no longer was just a crude power puncher but was now a more potent and poised champion.

The victory, itself, was somewhat tarnished by the severity of McClellan's injuries but it also showed that Benn was a more polished and mature champion at this stage of his career.

Benn returned to the ring and did not appear gun-shy at all, when he pounded out an 8th round technical knockout win over tough Italian Vincenzo Nardiello in July of 1995 in London, England.

In September of 1995 Benn stopped Danny Perez in 7 rounds in London, England, for another successful defense of his super middleweight title.

In March of 1996 Benn lost his title on a split decision in a rematch with the elusive and crafty Thulane Malinga in Newcastle, England. Malinga's ring style always presented a problem for Benn and both of their fights were extremely close.

In July of 1996 Benn decided to challenge World Boxing Organization champion Steve Collins for the title.

It was apparent that Benn was now past his prime as he was stopped by Collins in the 4th round in Manchester, England.

Benn asked Collins for a rematch with the title at stake again. The rematch was set, again, for November of 1996 in Manchester, England.

This time, Benn lasted until the 6th round before he was stopped by Collins again. Benn wisely retired from the ring after this loss.

The draw verdict in the Eubank rematch and the savage win over Gerald McClellan were probably the highlights of Benn's fistic career.

Benn is noted for his charity work and work with at-risk youth. He also works with Christian Groups counseling individuals with addictions.

In the 2003 issue of Ring Magazine Benn was listed as the 91st greatest puncher of all time in the history of the ring

Benn was entered into the World Boxing Council Hall of Fame in 2013.

Benn's final ring record is 42 wins, with 5 losses, and 1 draw. He took 35 fights by knockout, giving him a knockout to win percentage of 83.3 percent.

Gennady (GGG) Golovkin
Sportnote.com

Inductee # 15   GENNADY (GGG) GOLOVKIN

Gennadiy Gennadye Golovkin was born on April 8, 1982, in what is now Kazakhstan — it was part of the Soviet Union at the time. His father was a Russian coal miner, and his mother an ethnic Korean.

Golovkin began boxing competitively in 1993 at age 11 and was winning local tournaments. He began competing for the Kazakhstani National Boxing team at age 18 and entered international events.

At the 2003 World Amateur Boxing Championships in Bangkok, Thailand, he won a gold medal by beating future two-time champion Matvey Korobov. He qualified for the Athens Olympics by winning a gold medal at the 2004 Asian Amateur Boxing Championships held in the Philippines. He gained a silver medal at the 2004 Summer Olympic games held in Athens, losing to Russian Gaydarbek Gaydarbekov in the final match.

Golovkin's final amateur ring record was 345 wins with just 5 losses. Golovkin turned professional in May of 2006 after signing with a German promotional group named Universum.

Golovkin knocked out Gabor Balogh in one round in Dusseldorf, Germany in May of 2006. Then, over the next 3 years Golovkin honed his fighting skills by knocking out most of his opponents and going unbeaten in 18 professional fights.

Golovkin eventually terminated his contract with Universum because he felt they were more interested in promoting other fighters in their stable, which included Felix Sturm and Hassan N'Dam N'Jikam. Universum also incurred financial problems when they were dropped by German television channel ZDF.

As soon as Golovkin cut ties with Universum in January of 2010, the World Boxing Association issued an interim middleweight title fight between Golovkin and Milton Nunez. Rising to the challenge in August of 2010, Golovkin knocked out Nunez in just 58 seconds of the 1st round to win his first professional championship in his 19th professional fight in Panama City, Panama.

In December of 2010 Golovkin was upgraded to the regular middleweight title when he knocked out Nilson Julio Tapia in 3 rounds in Kazakhstan.

Golovkin returned to Panama in June of 2011 to knock out Kassim Ouma in 10 rounds to defend his World Boxing Association middleweight belt.

In December of 2011 Golovkin added the International Boxing Organization middleweight belt to his laurels when he knocked out LaJuan Simon in the first round in Dusseldorf, Germany.

In May of 2012 Golovkin defended both his middleweight belts by knocking out Makoto Fuchigami in 3 rounds in Kyiv, Ukraine.

In September of 2012 Golovkin fought for the first time in the United States when he put his World Boxing Association and International Boxing Organization middleweight title belts on the line against the European Grzegorz Proksa.

The match in the United States was arranged by K2 promotions, his new promotional team. Golovkin began training in Big Bear, California, for the fight under the guidance of trainer Abel Sanchez.

Sanchez noticed that Golovkin had a hard stinging jab and potent right cross. Sanchez instructed Golovkin on how to throw harder hooks to the body and to be more aggressive. Golovkin developed more of a hybrid style of fighting after working with Sanchez. It was a combination of a classic European style mixed with an aggressive Mexican style. Golovkin also picked up the nickname GGG for the first letters in his full name.

Golovkin was impressive in his American debut at Verona, New York, in January of 2013, when he knocked Proksa out in the 5th round. This was very significant as it was the first fight where Proksa had ever been knocked out.

Proksa also stated that Golovkin had incredible power for a middleweight. This was the 5th defense of Golovkin's World Boxing Association and International Boxing Organization middleweight titles.

In March of 2013 Golovkin stopped Nobuhiro Ishida out in 3 rounds in Monaco. Astonishingly, this was the first time Ishida had been knocked out in his 13-year ring career.

In June of 2013 Golovkin destroyed former British title challenger Matthew Macklin with a left hook to the body in the 3rd round in Ledyard, Connecticut.

In November of 2013 Golovkin took on top-ranked middleweight Curtis Stevens at an event broadcast to over 100 countries from Madison Square Garden in New York.

Golovkin dropped Stevens in the 2nd round with left hooks to the head, and Steven's corner finally threw in the towel to stop the carnage in the 8th round.

Next up for the Kazakhstani knockout machine was Osumanu Adama in February of 2014 in Monaco. Adama was ranked number 12 by the World Boxing Association. A hard left hook to the jaw in the 7th round forced the referee to stop the fight and award it to Golovkin.

In June of 2014 the World Boxing Association elevated Golovkin's status from Regular middleweight champion to Super middleweight champion. This was due to the fact that Golovkin had made 10 successful title defenses.

In July of 2014 Golovkin returned to Madison Square Garden to take on the number one ranked Ring middleweight Daniel Geale. Geale's record was 30 wins and 2 losses. Golovkin dropped Geale in the 2nd round and stopped him in the 3rd round for an easy defense of his Middleweight World Boxing Association and International Boxing Organization titles.

In October of 2014 Golovkin defended his titles and fought Marco Antonio Rubio for his interim World Boxing Council middleweight title in Carson, California.

In the 2nd round, Golovkin landed an overhand left to Rubio's head knocking him into the ropes and then down to the canvas. Rubio took the 10-count and then got up and claimed he was hit on the back of the head. The referee disallowed his claims of foul and awarded Golovkin a 2nd round knockout victory.

In February of 2015 Golovkin returned to Monaco to defend his belts against Martin Murray. Murray proved to be a durable opponent as he made it to 50 seconds of the 11th round before he was stopped in the fight.

In May of 2015 Golovkin defended his titles against Willie Monroe Junior in the Inglewood Forum in California. Golovkin stopped the game Monroe in the 6th round of the 12-round fight

In October of 2015 Golovkin defended his belts against International Boxing Federation Canadian champion David Lemieux.

GGG knocks out David Lemieux for the IBF middleweight title
The Sporting News 10/17/05

Lemieux was, like Golovkin, noted for his punching power. Golovkin's jab kept Lemieux off balance and he was dropped in the 5th round by a body shot. The referee saved Lemieux in the 8th round as he was unquestionably being battered. Golovkin also picked up Lemieux's International Boxing Federation middleweight title as a result of their match.

In April of 2016 Golovkin took on undefeated number one ranked International Boxing Federation challenger Dominic Wade at the Inglewood Forum. Golovkin made short work of Wade as he dropped him 3 times and stopped him in the 2nd round of the 12-round contest.

In September of 2016 Golovkin defended against undefeated

British International Boxing Federation welterweight champion Kell Brook in London, England.

Brook put up a tough fight against Golovkin and hit him with some clean punches. The fighters were about even on the scorecards when Brook had to retire in the 5th round due to a damaged eye socket. Golovkin was the winner, but he did not dominate the bout against the smaller welterweight contender. Brook would state after the fight that he had double and triple vision because of the damaged eye socket.

In March of 2017 Golovkin defended his belts against regular World Boxing Association champion Daniel Jacobs in Madison Square Garden in New York City.

Golovkin had to go the full 12 rounds to defeat Jacobs in a competitive fight. Jacobs was dropped in the 4th round, and Golovkin won by judges scores of 115-112 twice, and 114-113 on another judge's scorecard. Golovkin appeared to have solid ring control during the whole fight. This fight ended Golovkin's 23 fight knockout streak which had started in November of 2008.

The fight that everyone had been waiting for was finally made in September of 2017. Golovkin was finally going to fight Mexican legend Canelo Alvarez for all the middleweight belts in Las Vegas, Nevada.

Golovkin established his jab in the opening rounds. The action heated up in the middle rounds with Golovkin appearing to finish the rounds the stronger of the two. Both fighters went all out in the final 4 rounds with Golovkin appearing to finish slightly stronger than Alvarez. The decision by the judges was a split draw.

Most of the ringside press fight commentators felt that Golovkin won a close decision. Golovkin did manage to hold onto all of his belts due to the draw verdict.

Golovkin returned to the ring in May of 2018 with all of his belts intact when he took on the last-minute substitute Vanes Martirosyan in Las Vegas, Nevada. Golovkin easily knocked out Martirosyan in the 2nd round with 9 unanswered power punches which dropped him face first on the canvas for the full count.

The rematch with Canelo Alverez took place almost a year to the day in September of 2018. Alvarez won a disputed majority decision to take Golovkin's belts. The decision was disputed by fans and the media alike. As in the first fight, Golovkin appeared to do just enough to win a decision but the judges in Nevada always seemed to give Alvarez the edge in close fights due to his huge Mexican fan base.

Golovkin returned to the ring and stopped Canadian Steve Rolls in 4 rounds at Madison Square Garden in June of 2019. A left hook to the chin dropped Rolls face first onto the ring floor and he failed to beat the 10-count.

In October of 2019 Golovkin took on Ukrainian Sergiy Derevyanchenko for the vacant International Boxing Federation and International Boxing Organization middleweight titles in Madison Square Garden.

Golovkin dropped the Ukrainian with a 6-punch combination in the 1st round. Derevyanchenko fought back to even up the round. The two warriors fought at a fast pace for the whole 12 rounds, taking turns staggering each other. Golovkin walked away with a close unanimous decision to win his two belts back. Golovkin blamed illness for not being in top form for the fight.

In December of 2020 Golovkin defended his belts against Kamil Szeremeta in Hollywood, Florida. Golovkin gave Szeremeta a systematic beating before stopping him in the 7th round of the title fight.

Golovkin took 2 years off from the ring and returned in April of 2022 to defend his World Boxing Association and International Boxing Organization belts against Ryota Murata in Saitama, Japan. The World Boxing Association Super middleweight championship belt was also on the line.

Golovkin started out slow as Murata piled up points in the early rounds. Golovkin picked up the pace in the middle rounds and began hurting Murata before Murata's corner threw in the towel of surrender in the 9th round.

In September of 2022 Golovkin signed to fight Canelo Alvarez in the last fight of their trilogy. The fight took place in Las Vegas, Nevada, and the bout was to be contested at the super middleweight limit.

Golovkin finally appeared to have lost a step at age 40 when he lost a close 12-round decision to Alvarez. The verdict in this match appeared to be justified according to most ring experts. In 2023 Golovkin vacated all of his middleweight titles and has not fought since.

Golovkin now lives in Santa Monica, California, with his family and was training in nearby Big Bear, California. It is currently unknown if he will continue his ring career.

In my opinion there is no doubt that Golovkin has been the most prolific puncher in the middleweight division in the past 25 years. After reviewing their fights, in his 3-bout series with Canelo Alvarez, I believe that he won the first two fights and lost a close decision in the rubber match.

Both Golovkin and Alvarez are, no doubt, future hall of fame fighters who could punch and also had chins that were made of iron.

I believe that Golovkin probably peaked in his career about

the time he fought Alvarez the second time and he was slightly past his prime for the second and third bout with Alvarez.

Golovkin was as close to a perfect fighter as any knowledgeable ring observer can ever remember. Golovkin had a perfect blend of balance and extreme power in both fists. Stories of Golovkin's training sessions against huge heavyweights is the stuff that legends are made of.

Golovkin's current ring record is 42 wins,2 losses, and 1 ` draw. He has won 37 fights by knockout for a knockout to win ratio of 88.1 per cent. There is no doubt that Golovkin will be enshrined into the International Boxing Hall of Fame, soon after his announced retirement.

BIBLIOGRAPHY

Information from the following publications was used in preparation for this book.

The Ring magazine, September 1949

Boxing Yearbook, 1954

The Ring magazine, October 1954

Somebody up their likes me by Rocky Graziano, 1955

Boxing and Wrestling, July 1955

The Ring magazine, February 1956

Boxing Illustrated, June 1960

The Ring magazine, October 1961

Boxing International-All Star Wrestling, July 1965

Legendary Champions, by Rex Lardner, 1972

International Boxing, February 1973

The World Heavyweight Championship by J.D. McCallum, 1974

World Boxing, March 1976

The Ring record book, 1980

Sports Illustrated, October 18, 1982

KO magazine, November 1984

The Ring magazine, June 1988

Boxing 89, November 1989

Boxing Scene, January 1990

KO magazine, September 1990

The Ring magazine, October 1990

KO magazine, February 1991

The Ring magazine, February 1993

The Ring magazine, July 1994

Boxing 94, November 1994

The Ring magazine, July 1995

The Ring magazine, September 1998

The Ring Yearbook, 100 greatest punchers, 2003

The Killings of Stanley Ketchel, James Carlos Blake, 2005

KO presents boxing, 2006

The Sporting News, October 17, 2015 Steven Muehlhausen

The Illinois Thunderbolt, Larry Carli, 2016

Ring News 24, Eric Armit, November 2023

Boxrec.com

Sportnote.com

ACKNOWLEDGEMENTS

This book would not have been possible without the help and guidance of the following people.

Aaron Lingenfelter, Chief Editor

Max G. McClendon, Historical Research

Rochelle Cody, Cover Design, and Graphics

About the Author

The author, Larry Carli is a retired Sheriff Detective and District Attorney Criminal investigator from Sacramento County, California. He has published four books titled, The Illinois Thunderbolt, the life story of boxer Billy Papke, The Top Ten Middleweight Champions of All Time, Boxing's Super 70's, and 1950's Boxing in Black and White.

The author has a master's degree in Criminal Justice and Research from the University of Alabama and is also a former member of the International Boxing Research Organization, the National Sportscasters and Sports writers Association, and the California Writers Club.

www.ingramcontent.com/pod-product-compliance
Lightning Source LLC
Chambersburg PA
CBHW060802110426
42739CB00032BA/2555